The Art of Lisp Programming

Robin Jones   Clive Maynard   Ian Stewart

The Art of Lisp Programming

With 12 Illustrations

Springer-Verlag
London Berlin Heidelberg New York
Paris Tokyo Hong Kong

Robin Jones
Department of Mathematics, Science and Information Technology,
South Kent College, Folkestone CT20 2NA, UK

Clive Maynard
School of Electrical and Computer Engineering, Curtin University of
Technology, Perth, W. Australia

Ian Stewart
Mathematics Institute, University of Warwick, Coventry CV4 7AL,
UK

The illustrations by Sir John Tenniel that decorate all chapters except for the Quick Reference Guide are reproduced from *Alice's Adventures in Wonderland* and *Through the Looking-Glass* by Lewis Carroll, with the permission of the publishers, MacMillan & Co. Ltd., London.

ISBN 3–540–19568–8 Springer-Verlag Berlin Heidelberg New York
ISBN 0–387–19568–8 Springer-Verlag New York Berlin Heidelberg

British Library of Cataloguing in Publication Data
Jones, Robin
  The art of lisp programming.
  1. Computer systems. programming languages: Lisp languages
  I. Title II. Maynard, Clive, *1945–* III. Stewart, Ian, *1944–*
  005.13'3
  ISBN 3-540-19568-8

Library of Congress Cataloging-in-Publication Data
Jones, Robin
  The art of Lisp programming/Robin Jones, Clive Maynard, Ian Stewart,
    p. cm.
  ISBN 0-387-19568-8 (U.S.)
  1. LISP (Computer Program language) I. Maynard, Clive, *1944–* II. Stewart, Ian.
  III. Title.
QA76.73.L23J66   1989
005.13'3--dc20   89-21706 CIP

Filmset by Goodfellow and Egan
Printed by The Alden Press Ltd, Osney Mead, Oxford
543210 – Printed on acid-free paper.

"What does it live on?" Alice asked, with great curiosity.
"Sap and sawdust," said the Gnat. "Go on with the list."

Lewis Carroll, *Through the Looking-Glass*

Preface

Until recently, Lisp was a language used largely by the Artificial Intelligentsia on mainframe computers. The existing textbooks are consequently directed at a sophisticated audience. But over the last few years Lisp has become widely available on IBM PCs, Macintoshes and the like. Furthermore, Lisp is an immensely powerful general-purpose language. The aim of this book is to introduce the philosophy and features of the language to new users in a simple and accessible fashion.

The reader is likely to be familiar with several procedural languages such as Pascal or BASIC, but may not have met a functional language before. Lisp is a good starting point for learning about such languages. Functional languages in general are beginning to become popular because their mathematically oriented structure makes them more susceptible to formal methods of program proof than are procedural languages. It's an important practical problem to prove that software actually does what it's designed to do—especially if, as is not unusual, it's controlling an ICBM with a 50-megaton warhead. In addition, functional languages are attractive for parallel programming, the hardware for which is now becoming available at realistic costs.

Our main objective is to present the basic ideas of Lisp, without too many confusing frills, so that the reader gets used to the particular style of thinking required in a functional programming language. This is precisely why we *don't* use some of the standard techniques. For example, our program layout is unconventional: the aim is to emphasize the logical structure of the code rather than to save space. While developing the facility to program in Lisp we solve some problems before having introduced the most appropriate tools. To the experienced programmer the resulting code will look clumsy—and, we hope, to you when you've finished the book—but the sheer fact that we can do this illustrates the flexibility of the language. It also gives some insight into how the standard functions might be constructed.

This book is not a reference manual. Although it standardizes on Common Lisp, it discusses only a fraction of the full range of functions in that implementation of the language. It's a question of seeing the wood for the trees: the new user would find the full language bafflingly complex. We hope that, by the time the reader has finished this book, his manuals will have become accessible.

Where appropriate, chapters end with a series of exercises. We have given answers immediately after them, because the material forms an integral part of the development of the reader's understanding of the language.

The early chapters develop the language using short, easily understood functions. However, not all Lisp is short, or easily understood. To give a feeling for what a realistic project might look like, the last three chapters develop a Lisp-based interpreter for the language ABC.

Most Lisp systems have an interpreter and a compiler. We confine our attention to interpreters, because they provide instant feedback and, usually, simple editing features. The reader will get most out of the book by working through it while sitting in front of a warm computer running a Lisp interpreter.

Thus far we have referred to ourselves in the plural. However, only one of us wrote any particular chapter, so to continue to do so strikes us as stilted and formal. Henceforward 'we' therefore becomes 'I'. Any reader who dislikes this should invoke Lisp's power and

```
( defmacro I() 'we )
```

Folkestone, Kent   Robin Jones
Perth, W. Australia   Clive Maynard
Coventry, Warwickshire   Ian Stewart

Contents

· 1 ·
Some Basic Ideas

The White Rabbit put on his spectacles. "Where shall I begin, please your Majesty?" he asked.

"Begin at the beginning", the King said, very gravely, "and go on till you come to the end: then stop."

Alice's Adventures in Wonderland

There are those who will tell you that LISP is an acronym for LISt Processor and others who insist that it stands for Lots of Infuriatingly Silly Parentheses. Both camps have good arguments to back them up. Lisp *is* a language which deals almost exclusively in list structures, and there are a great many brackets in a typical Lisp program. Paradoxically, Lisp derives much of its power as a programming language from the fact that it *is* limited in this way, and, as we shall see, this philosophy leads automatically to the proliferation of similar symbols (which just happen to be brackets) which so incense Lisp's detractors.

Lists

Perhaps we should begin, then, by studying what is meant by the term 'list' in the current context, and try to see why a list is such a powerful construct.

Suppose that you are writing a word processor. A simple technique for storing the text in memory would be to use an array as shown in Figure 1. There are two main objections to this rather naive format. First, an attempt to add the word 'black' before 'cat' requires that the remaining words in the text are each

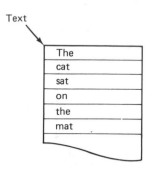

FIGURE 1. How not to store text.

shuffled one cell down the array. This is OK if we're talking about a six word sentence, as here, but if it's the first sentence of the great American novel, there's going to be a long wait before the extra adjective is successfully inserted. Second, there's an implicit assumption that all words are of the same length. Of course, a word may be padded with spaces, but that will waste memory, and there's certainly a limit to the size of word which can be held. So let's consider an alternative arrangement, shown in Figure 2. Here, each entry consists of a word and a pointer to the next entry. The physical order of the entries no longer matters, so that additional words can be added to the text simply by creating cells for them and altering a couple of pointers (see Figure 3).

That deals neatly with the editing problem, but it still leaves us with the difficulty of handling what are effectively fixed-length words. Suppose we revise the structure of Figure 3 so that each entry consists not of a datum plus a pointer, but *two* pointers. Now the left-hand pointer can point to a similar structure which identifies a word and of course it can be any length, because we can signal

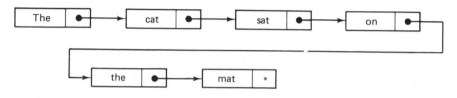

FIGURE 2. A better structure.

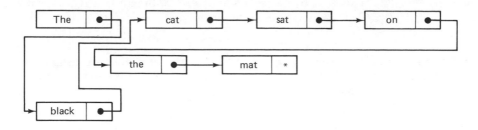

FIGURE 3. Adding the word 'black' now only entails some pointer manipulation.

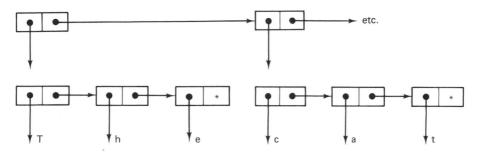

FIGURE 4. A true list. Now words can be indefinitely long.

its end with some appropriate delimiting value for the pointer. We now have the organization shown in Figure 4, where the delimiting pointer is an asterisk.

It's clear that this is an immensely flexible structure, because there is nothing in principle to prevent us from extending it indefinitely. Each pair of pointers may point to other structures of the same general type, or to terminating symbols. In this example, such symbols are either letters or null pointers, but there are all sorts of other possibilities. Note, however, that while both pointers can point to other structures, only left pointers can point to terminal symbols and only right pointers can be null.

The structures we have been discussing are called lists. The terminal symbols (here letters) are called *atoms*, because clearly they cannot be divided further. (Yes, I *know* physicists are always splitting them, but that's their fault for choosing the word before finding out that they could do so. We will use the word with its original meaning.)

Representing Lists

Clearly, the diagrammatic notation for a list of Figure 4 is inappropriate to a computer language, although there are occasions when it can be a useful prop on which to hang an idea and I shall use it from time to time in this book. Lisp employs a simple symbolic notation. For example, the list of letters 'A,B,C,D' is written (A B C D) and can be visualized as Figure 5. Similarly, Figure 6 shows the list ((a b) (c d e)). The Lisp form of the complete list of Figure 4 would be:

((T h e) (c a t) (s a t) (o n) (t h e) (m a t))

Note that spaces are used to separate atoms, but are otherwise insignificant. Thus the spaces between brackets and those between brackets and atoms are not necessary but do no harm.

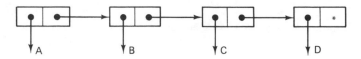

FIGURE 5. (A B C D).

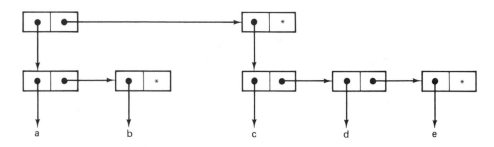

FIGURE 6. ((a b) (c d e)).

The Interpreter

We're very nearly in a position actually to try something out. Enter your Lisp interpreter. The syntax for this will be implementation dependent, but it will probably involve invoking an executable file from disk, perhaps coupled with an environment file. In any event, you should be greeted with a prompt which is likely to be '>'.

It should come as no surprise that the interpreter will only accept atoms or lists as input. So let's give it a list. Type:

         ( )

The interpreter will probably respond as soon as it sees the closing bracket (but some implementations require you to hit RETURN):

    NIL

What's happened is this. The interpreter has accepted the list, which is empty, and immediately *evaluated* it. Its value is NIL, which is a reserved Lisp atom meaning *either* the empty list or the logical value FALSE. Since we're at the top level of the interpreter, Lisp has returned this value to us.

Functions

Now let's be a little more ambitious. Type:

    (+ 3 7)

Lisp will respond:

    10

This time the list which we have presented to the interpreter consists of a *function* name (+) together with a series of *arguments* on which the function is to operate (3 and 7). Fortunately, the function is a *primitive* (i.e. it is built-in and does not have to be defined by the user) so Lisp knows what to do with the arguments. It does the business and returns the result (10).

So a Lisp function call is a list which consists of a function name and a set of arguments. It returns a result according to the definition of the function. The number of arguments may or may not be determined by the function in question. For example, we can write:

    (+ 3 5 2 5 3)

and confidently expect the interpreter to announce:

    18

If, however, I were to write a function called **dec** whose purpose is to decrement a value by one, it is evident that it could take only one argument.

At the moment I could not write:

    (dec 6)

without incurring the displeasure of the interpreter, because the function does not yet exist. We shall see how to write it shortly. I could *never* write:

    (dec 8 9)

because, from my definition of what dec is to do, it can't make sense, and the interpreter will know that.

Two More Primitives

So far, we've met a single primitive function, '+', whose use is self explanatory. There's an equally obvious one to do subtraction (−).

Now, to tell Lisp about my new function **dec**, I clearly need to be able to say, "Don't try to evaluate this, because you don't know about it yet. Rather, store it as a definition for future use." Lisp provides a function called **defun** for doing this. **defun** takes as arguments the name of the function to be defined, a list of arguments, and a list which represents the action which the function is to take. (Actually, this is a slightly woolly definition, not least because **defun** isn't really a function at all. However, it *looks* like one. We shall treat anything that looks like a function as though it is one for the time being. This will do us no lasting harm.)

So a definition of **dec** looks like this:

```
( defun dec ( x )
      ( - x 1 )
)
```

The layout is a matter of personal choice. I could just as well have written:

```
( defun dec ( x )( - x 1 ) )
```

but it's clear that, even in this simple case, keeping track of the brackets needs some attention, and in more complex cases the chances of getting a valid expression first time are proportional to the neatness and consistency of your layout.

If you type this in, the interpreter will respond:

```
DEC
```

So **defun** returns the name of the function which has been defined. Now the new function can be used by writing:

```
( dec 6 )
```

for instance, and the response will be:

```
5
```

Constants and Variables

In the above example, I've mixed constants and variables without comment. This is because the representation is so similar to that for any other common computer language. That is, where I have used a letter (x) the interpreter assumes I mean it to be a variable and where a number appears it's taken as a constant. What happens if I *want* the letter x to be treated as a constant we shall duck for the time being.

S-Expressions

There is only one more piece of terminology which need concern us at this stage. An S-expression (short for symbolic expression) is any valid Lisp expression consisting of atoms and brackets. Obviously, a sequence of characters in which the brackets do not match isn't an S-expression. The same is true of a sequence which does not begin with an open bracket (unless it's just an atom) but there are other possibilities which I'll temporarily defer.

Postscript

This chapter has introduced almost all of the fundamental features of Lisp, although it will not yet be clear how they can be used. However, what should be evident is that the language has a remarkable consistency, built around very few basic constructs. For instance, the basic structure is the list; functions are themselves lists and there is a function (which is, of course, a list) for defining other functions. This means that more and more complex functions can be built from the primitives and, in effect, the language becomes more powerful in the process.

Also, since both data and functions are lists, there is no significant boundary between them, so that it is possible to treat a program as data and modify it during execution.

Again, because of the list organization, it is simple to have functions which take indefinitely many arguments (as + does), a feature which many languages find a particularly difficult hurdle.

Exercises 1

1.1 Define a function **sq** (x) which returns the square of x.

1.2 Using **sq**, define a function **diff** $(x\ y)$ which returns $x^2\text{-}y^2$.

1.3 According to elementary algebra, $x^2\text{-}y^2 = (x+y)(x-y)$. How would you write the right-hand side in Lisp?

1.4 Define a function called **test** $(x\ y)$ which returns 0 if **diff** $(x\ y)$ is equal to $(x+y)(x-y)$.

1.5 What is the biggest product of two integers which your Lisp implementation will evaluate correctly? Why do you think this is?

1.6 The ancient Babylonians computed products xy by using tables of squares and the identity:

$$4xy = (x+y)^2 - (x-y)^2 \tag{1}$$

which implies:

$$xy = ((x+y)^2 - (x-y)^2)/4 \tag{2}$$

Write a function **forprod** $(x\ y)$ to evaluate the right-hand side of (1) using only **sq** and the arithmetic primitives. Use it to write a function **babyprod** $(x\ y)$ that evaluates the right-hand side of (2). Write a function **check** $(x\ y)$ that divides (**babyprod** $x\ y$) by xy, and use it to verify that (**babyprod** 12 13) = 156.

Answers

1.1   (defun sq (x)
              (* x x)
)

1.2   (defun diff (x y)
              (- (sq x) (sq y))
)

1.3   (* (+ x y) (- x y))

```
1.4     ( defun test ( x y )
            ( - ( diff x y )
                ( * ( + x y ) ( - x y ) ) )
            )
        )
```

1.5 On mine it is 32767. It thinks that 16384 * 2 = −32768. I deduce that it uses a 16-bit integer in 2's complement notation, since $32768 = 2^{15}$.

```
1.6     ( defun forprod ( x y )
            ( - ( sq ( + x y ) ) ) ( sq ( - x y ) ) )
        )
        ( defun babyprod ( x y )
            ( / ( forprod x y ) 4 )
        )
        ( defun check ( x y )
            ( / ( babyprod x y ) ( * x y ) ) )
        )
```

· 2 ·

List Functions

The players all played at once, without waiting for turns, quarreling all the while, and fighting for the hedgehogs; and in a very short time the Queen was in a furious passion, and went stamping about, and shouting "Off with his head!" or "Off with her head!" about once in a minute.

Alice's Adventure in Wonderland

It will not have escaped your attention that, while I spent the whole of Chapter 1 extolling the virtues of lists as data structures, I omitted to mention any Lisp primitives for handling them. I shall remedy that now.

Splitting Lists

It's fairly obvious that we need some mechanism for decomposing a list into its constituent parts. If we use the graphical realization of a list shown in, for example, Figure 6, it should be clear that a simple technique would be to separate the two pointers at the top left. The first points to the left sublist (*a b*), and the second points to a pointer which identifies the right sublist (*c d e*). A sensible way of referring to these entities would be to talk about the head of the list (*a b*), and the tail of the list (*c d e*). Note that, under this definition, the head of a list may be an atom. For instance, in Figure 5 it is the atom *A*; but it can be a list, as here.

Let's decompose the list of Figure 6 a stage further to get a clearer idea of the operations that are legal. We'll call the head s (i.e. $s = (a\ b)$).

So the head of s is the atom a; its tail is the *list* (*b*). We cannot now take the head of the head of s (i.e. the head of an atom)—the concept is meaningless. We *can* take the head of the tail; the result is the *atom b*. The tail of the tail of s yields the empty list, NIL.

Just as we cannot take the head of an atom, the tail of an atom makes no sense either. There is, however, one special case to consider; it is always legitimate to take the head or the tail of NIL. The result is still NIL. Although this rule *appears* to create a little inconsistency in Lisp, it doesn't really. Remember that NIL is *either* the empty list or an atom meaning FALSE, so Lisp can simply assume that, if it's asked to take the head of NIL, the former description is the one which is currently in force. This means that the tail of a list may be taken indefinitely many times and sooner or later the result will be NIL, but the process can then continue to be repeated without causing an error.

car and cdr

Lisp has functions which model the operations I have called **head** and **tail**. They are called **car** and **cdr**. The nomenclature is a throw-back to the assembly mnemonics of the IBM 709 on which Lisp was first developed. (They split an address word into two parts—obviously very useful in this context.) For some reason, the notation has stuck, but it doesn't follow that we are stuck with it. For example, I could write:

```
( defun head ( x )
     ( car x )
)
```

and:

```
( defun tail ( x )
     ( cdr x )
)
```

Now **head** and **tail** are synonyms for **car** and **cdr**. I shall assume that you have included these two function definitions in all the code in the first part of this book, so that I can continue to use **head** and **tail**, terms which are, after all, rather more meaningful.

Setting Up Lists

I can now return to a problem that I referred to briefly in Chapter 1, namely, the constant/variable distinction. In fact, the problem is wider than in most computer languages because almost any symbol may stand for a wide range of objects.

For example, in BASIC, if I write $B\$$, the system is immediately aware that this is a variable of type 'string', unless it's included in quote marks, in which case it's a literal. But in Lisp, is x a numeric variable, the letter 'x', or a list variable? Also, if x is a variable, how can I assign a value to it?

Let's answer those questions in reverse order. I can't have an assignment statement, like BASIC or Pascal, because there *are* no statements in Lisp, only functions.

setq

Obviously, then, we need a function that models the familiar assignment operation. It's called **setq** (for SET Quote). You'll see the reason for this rather obscure terminology shortly. I prefer to think about it as SET Quantity. Anyway:

```
( setq x 1 )
```

assigns the value 1 to the variable x, much as '$x = 1$' would in BASIC. There are two important differences though. First, **setq**, being a function, *returns* something. In this case that is 1, the assigned value. Second (and this answers the first question), Lisp takes its cue about the type of a variable from the data being assigned to it. So x is assumed to be a number.

Let's consider some more examples:

```
( setq y x )
```

evidently assigns the value of x to y (i.e. y becomes 1). Suppose that we want y to have the value x though. There is a function, **quote**, which returns its own argument, to do this:

```
( setq y ( quote x ) )
```

which we could see as equivalent to a BASIC statement $y = $ "x", except, of course, that y would have to be a string variable. This construction is needed so often that a less unwieldy form is implemented:

```
( setq y 'x )
```

This suggests that it should have been possible to write:

```
( setq x '1 )
```

to set x to 1. You can do this; the only reason the quote mark is unnecessary is that Lisp can deduce that 1 cannot be a variable. It does so by employing the same rule as most common languages in this context, namely variable names must start with a letter. Incidentally, they may be indefinitely long and may contain special characters.

Assigning a list to a variable is now easy. For instance:

```
( setq fig_6 '( ( a b ) ( c d e ) ) )
```

would set the variable fig_6 to the list of Figure 6.

A Piece of Pedantry

In the above discussion, I've been playing fast and loose with the term *function*, a sin which I also admitted in Chapter 1. I'll clarify the point now. In the strict mathematical sense, a function accepts a set of values (arguments), performs some set of operations on them and returns exactly *one* value as a result. This must be the case because it is the function *itself* which attains the returned value. However, **setq**, while behaving like a function in that it returns a value, also performs an assignment. In other words it has a *side effect*, which, as it happens, is more important than the fact that it returns something. The same is true of **defun**, which only returns the function name, but whose most useful effect is to store a function definition.   Strictly, **setq** and **defun** are consequently not functions. They may be called procedures, and a procedure can be simply thought of as a function with a side effect.

Head and Tail Revisited

The **head** and **tail** functions need a little more thought than might be appreciated when the argument list is nontrivial. To see why, use the **setq** function above to set up the list:

```
( ( a b ) ( c d e ) )
```

Now try (head fig_6). You'll get the response (a b)—no surprise here. But what about (tail fig_6)? This time you get ((c d e)) when you might have expected just (c d e). All is explained if you look carefully at the list's diagrammatic representation. The head is a pointer to the list (a b), but the tail is a pointer to a pointer to the list (c d e). Hence the 'extra' pair of brackets. The list (c d e) is:

```
( head ( tail fig_6 ) )
```

Similarly:

```
( tail ( tail fig_6 ) ) returns NIL
```

and:

```
( tail ( head ( tail fig_6 ) ) ) returns ( d e )
```

Incidentally, if you've been following all this on your machine, you'll have noticed that Lisp does not distinguish between upper and lower case variable and function names, and treats everything as upper case. So, for instance, the last result would actually show up as (D E) with all unnecessary spaces removed. Most programmers, myself included, tend to work in lower case regardless, because we don't like to shout at computers. Also, we can then use upper case in listings to identify special symbols or atoms like NIL.

cons

We'll leave the problem of analysing lists for the moment and consider the inverse problem of synthesizing them. The function **cons** returns a list constructed from its two arguments, which will then be the head and tail of the resultant list. For example:

```
( setq h 'a )
( setq ta '( b c d ) )
( cons h ta )
```

would return the list (a b c d). For the reasons examined in looking at the **head** and **tail** functions, it's clear that h may be an atom or a list, but ta must be a list, even if it's only NIL. (You may wonder why I've used h and ta rather than h and t above; you'll see in Chapter 3.)

We can also see that:

```
( cons ( head list ) ( tail list ) )
```

will return list, whatever that was.

Postscript

Amazingly, these are the only functions necessary to do any operations we like on lists. Most versions of Lisp implement more complex functions to simplify particularly common processes. For instance, the function caar is often used for 'head of head of'. I shall not, however, assume the presence of such functions so as to minimize compatibility problems. We shall develop our own versions as and when we need them.

Exercises 2

Questions 1–5 are about a simple database for names and addresses. This takes the form of a list which we shall call *directory*, obtained by repeatedly applying **cons** to lists of the form (name address). In turn, name and address are atoms.

For example, with entries:

```
NAME                ADDRESS
Eeyore              The-Gloomy-Place
Piglet              The-Beech-Tree
Owl                 The-Chestnuts
```

directory becomes:

```
( ( ( Eeyore The-Gloomy-Place )
    ( Piglet The-Beech-Tree    )
  )
    ( Owl The-Chestnuts        )
)
```

2.1 Represent the above as a diagram.
2.2 How would you set up *directory* as shown above?

2.3 What combination of **head** and **tail** functions will return Piglet's address?

2.4 How would you add the list d4:

```
( Pooh-Bear Mr-Saunders )
```

to the end of the list? (Pooh Bear lived *under the name of* Mr. Saunders; that was written over his front door.)

2.5 Does:

```
( setq directory1 ( cons d4 directory ) )
```

add Pooh's entry to the list?

2.6 What does **ttail**, defined as follows, do?

```
( defun ttail ( x )
      ( tail (tail x ) )
)
```

What do you get when it is applied to directory?

2.7 Set up *four* to be the list (1 2 3 4). What combinations of head and tail return the atoms 1, 2, 3, 4?

2.8 Initialize *fred* with:

```
( setq fred '( (1 2) (3 4) ) )
```

What combinations of **head** and **tail** return atoms 1, 2, 3, 4?

2.9 Initialize *emily* with:

```
( setq emily '( (1 2) (3 4) (5 6 7) ) )
```

Which of the following produce error messages? Otherwise, what is returned?

    (a) (head(head(head emily)))
    (b) (head(head emily))
    (c) (head emily)
    (d) (tail(head emily))
    (e) (head(tail(head(tail emily))))

2.10 If *num* is (1 2 3), how can you obtain ((1 2 3)) using **cons**?

Answers

2.1

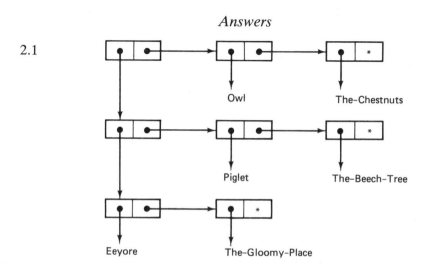

2.2
```
( setq n1 'Eeyore )
(setq n2 'Piglet )
( setq n3 'Owl )
( setq a1 'The-Gloomy-Place )
( setq a2 'The-Beech-Tree )
( setq a3 'The-Chestnuts )
( setq d1 (cons n1 a1) )
( setq d2 (cons n2 a2) )
( setq d3 (cons n3 a3) )
( setq dir1 (cons d1 d2) )
(setq directory (cons dir1 d3) )
```

2.3
```
( tail ( tail (head directory) ) )
```

2.4
```
( setq n4 'Pooh-Bear )
( setq d4 'Mr-Saunders )
( setq d4 (cons n4 d4) )
( setq directory (cons directory d4) )
```

2.5 Not really; the structure of directory is changed. Instead of

```
(((( Pooh-Bear Mr-Saunders ) ( Eeyore
     The-Gloomy-Place ))
     ( Piglet The-Beech-Tree ))
     ( Owl The-Chestnuts ))
```

    you get

```
(( Pooh-Bear Mr-Saunders) ((( Eeyore
     The-Gloomy-Place))
     (Piglet The-Beech-Tree))
     (Owl The-Chestnuts))
```

2.6 The tail of the tail of x.

```
(The-Chestnuts)
```

2.7
```
( setq four '(1 2 3 4) )
      1 = (head four)
      2 = ( head (tail four) )
      3 = ( head (tail (tail four) ) )
      4 = ( head ( tail ( tail (tail four) ) ) )
```

2.8
```
1 = ( head (head fred) )
2 = ( head ( tail (head fred) ) )
3 = ( head ( head (tail fred) ) )
4 = ( head ( tail ( head (tail fred) ) ) )
```

2.9   (a) error
       (b) 1
       (c) (1 2)
       (d) (2)
       (e) 4

2.10
```
( cons ( 1 2 3 ) NIL )
```

· 3 ·
Predicates

"All right so far," said the King; and he went on muttering over the verses to himself: " 'We know it to be true' ".

Alice's Adventures in Wonderland

No computer language can function at a level beyond the trivial without some mechanism for handling different processes under different conditions. Every procedural language you can think of has an 'IF' statement to do this. Lisp has no statements, so it can't have one called 'IF'. However, if you think about the mechanism employed in a statement like:

```
IF x = 3 THEN ....
```

the *expression* $x = 3$ is evaluated to TRUE or FALSE and the body of the statement is executed only if the result was TRUE. Clearly, Lisp could have *functions* that return these two logical values to do the same kind of job. It does, and they are called *predicates*. A predicate is a function that returns T or NIL. Now you know why I couldn't abbreviate 'tail' to 't' in Chapter 2. Lisp would have taken it as an attempt to alter the reserved atom T and complained. I have previously commented that NIL can mean FALSE. An example of a predicate which takes any Lisp object as an argument is **atom**. This returns T if the argument is an atom and NIL otherwise. So:

```
( setq x 'a )
( atom x )
```

will return T, but:

```
( atom fig_6 )
```

will return NIL.

An example of a predicate which can only be sensibly applied to numbers is **zerop**. This returns T only if its argument is zero. Thus:

```
( setq one 1 )
( zerop ( dec one ) )
```

would return T. Note the 'p' on the end of the function name to indicate that it is a predicate. You might reasonably ask why **atom** is not similarly terminated and the answer is "I don't know". However, there is a rather weak convention that numeric predicates have a 'p' as their last letter.

To say that zerop has a meaning only for a numeric argument implies that its use with a string or a list is illegal, which is generally the case. That means you have to be careful that the object you're testing really is of the type you think it is. Otherwise you may get some baffling results. There is a predicate **numberp** that can be used to confirm that an object is a number before testing for zero. But that raises a new question. How can we phrase a test like: "see if the object is a number and only if it is, test it for zero"?

cond

The solution is to use another function called **cond** (for condition). **Cond** takes a sequence of lists as its arguments, each consisting of a pair of functions, the first of which must be a predicate. In general, then, we could see it as something like this:

```
( cond
      ( p1 e1 )
      ( p2 e2 )
      ( p3 e3 )
          :
          :
      ( pn en )
)
```

where p1, p2, p3 etc. are predicates and e1, e2 and so on are *any* Lisp functions. **Cond** evaluates each predicate in turn until it finds one which returns T. It then returns the value of the function paired with it, and ignores all the subsequent functions. Thus if p1 and p2 are both NIL, but p3 is T, e3 is returned, regardless of p4, e4, p5, e5 and so on.

This is a neat and powerful mechanism. It is equivalent to a rather complex IF statement in BASIC which would read something like:

```
IF p1 THEN e1 ELSE IF p2 THEN e2 ELSE IF p3 THEN e3 ....
```

I'll illustrate its use by writing a function called **test** which will examine a single argument, return NUMBER if the argument is a number, ATOM if it's an atom other than a number, and the head of the list if it's anything else.

```
( defun test ( x )
    ( cond
          ( ( numberp x ) 'number )
          ( ( atom x )       'atom )
          ( T            ( head x ) )
    )
)
```

This bears a little explanation. Obviously, if *x* is a number, the atom NUMBER is returned, the function taking no further action. If not, the next test is performed and the result will be set to the atom ATOM if *x* is atomic. If neither of these conditions is met, the third predicate is evaluated. Because it is T, which is bound to be true, the value of the matching function is returned (i.e. the head of the argument list).

It's very common to see T as the final predicate in a COND function to act as a catch-all in this way. Also note that we can be confident that the 'head' function is not being performed on an atom, which would lead to an error message since it's illegal, because a return would already have been forced by the predicate (atom x) in that case.

Boolean Functions

Let's expand on these ideas a little by looking at how we could implement a set of Boolean functions. If you're unfamiliar with such operations, here's a brief summary of them, but if you've met digital logic before you can skip the next few paragraphs.

There are four basic logical operations called NOT, OR, AND and XOR. We'll assume (incorrectly but conveniently) that each except NOT takes two arguments, each of which can only be T or NIL. NOT only takes one argument. Each function returns another logical variable (i.e. T or NIL) according to the following rules:

NOT returns T if its argument is NIL and vice versa.
OR returns T if either of its arguments is T.
AND returns T only if both its arguments are T.
XOR returns T only if its arguments are different.

These operations represent the building blocks of all digital computer circuitry and I shall have more to say about that later.

There is a pretty fair chance that, with the exception of XOR, the functions are already present in your Lisp implementation and are given the above names. So if you want to test out what follows, you'll have to call our functions something different unless you want to confuse the interpreter and yourself. I'll choose the following notation:

NOT :˜
OR : V
AND : A

These symbols are fairly close to the mathematical standards for the same operations.

First the NOT function:

```
( defun ˜ ( x )
      (cond
            ( x NIL )
            ( T   T )
      )
)
```

That looks a bit weird, but it's perfectly logical (no pun intended); if x is T, NIL is returned, otherwise—and that must mean x is NIL—T is passed back. Here's OR:

```
( defun V ( x y )
      ( cond
            ( x T )
            ( T y )
      )
)
```

This time, if x is T, T is returned because it doesn't matter what y is. If not, the function is whatever y is. Now for AND:

```
(defun A ( x y )
      ( cond
            ( x y )
            ( T NIL )
      )
)
```

You should be getting the hang of this. If x is T the result is whatever y is. Otherwise it must be NIL. Finally, XOR:

```
( defun xor ( x y )
      ( cond
            ( ( A x y ) NIL )
            ( ( V x y ) T )
            ( T NIL )
      )
)
```

So if x AND y is T, the result must be NIL. If that isn't true, but x OR y is, the result is T. The only remaining condition is that both arguments are NIL, which returns NIL.

Exercises 3

3.1 The Boolean functions nand, nor, implies and iff are defined as follows:

p nand *q* = not (*p* and *q*)
p nor *q* = not (*p* or *q*)
p implies q = (not *p*) or *q*
p iff *q* = (*p* implies *q*) and (*q* implies *p*)

Write Lisp functions to mimic these.

Answers

3.1   (defun nand (x y)
           (~ (A x y))
)

     (defun nor (x y)
           (~ (V x y))
)

     (defun imp (x y)
           (V (~ x) y)
)

     (defun iff (x y)
           (A (imp x y) (imp y x))
)

·4·

Recursion

"Well, just then I was inventing a new way of getting over a gate—would you like to hear it?"

"Very much indeed," Alice said politely.

"I'll tell you how I came to think of it," said the Knight.

"You see, I said to myself 'The only difficulty is with the feet: the head is high enough already'. Now first I put my head on top of the gate—then the head's high enough—then I stand on my head—then the feet are high enough, you see—then I'm over you see."

Through the Looking-Glass

You will have noticed that I have not yet attempted to write a piece of code containing a loop. The reason for this is that it is often convenient not to use conventional iteration structures at all in Lisp. Such structures are implemented, but they aren't actually necessary. So I'm going to be somewhat puritanical and do without them entirely for the moment.

This may seem somewhat perverse. After all, few useful computational processes can be performed without repetition. However, looping and repetition are not quite the same thing. We can make a function execute repeatedly by simply allowing it to call itself. A function that does this is called *recursive*.

Here's the simplest possible (and totally useless) recursive function we could write:

```
( defun silly ( x )
    ( silly x )
)
```

A call to **silly** will invoke a call to **silly** which will call **silly** which will . . . Well, you get the idea. The process will continue until the end of the world, or, more likely, until the system runs out of memory. It will do so because it has to hold the housekeeping details of each incidence of the function call. None of these are ever deleted because the function never returns! What we need is a way to stop the recursion, just as we need a way of terminating a loop. Let's examine a concrete example to get a feel for the techniques involved.

Powers

Suppose I want to write a function **power** which takes two arguments x and n and evaluates x^n. Rule 1 is "Always consider the simplest case first". Here, that is x^0, which is 1. So a first stab at the function looks like this:

```
( defun power ( x n )
    ( cond
              ( ( zerop n )     1  )
              ( T   (then what?) )
    )
)
```

So far, then, we have tested n for zero and returned 1 if that was true. Promising, but clearly incomplete. What we need is a second more general relationship— one which tends towards the trivial result we have already dealt with. In this case the formula we want is:

$$p^n = p \times p^{n-1}$$

Of course, this is only one of many identities concerning powers that I could have written down. The significance of this one is that, repetitively applied, it will eventually lead to the known result.

For example,

$$p^3 = p \times p^2$$

$$p^2 = p \times p^1$$

$$p^1 = p \times p^0$$

and we already know that's 1. So the function becomes:

```
( defun power ( x n )
    ( cond
              ( ( zerop n )     1  )
              ( T       ( * x ( power x ( dec n ) ) ) ) )
    )
)
```

Boolean Functions Revisited

Let's apply the same kind of analysis to the Boolean functions I introduced in Chapter 3. You'll recall that I defined the AND and OR functions as having two arguments. This was an oversimplification which suited me at the time, but now we can afford to be more expansive. Each of these operations should be allowed to have an unlimited number of 'inputs'. In the case of AND, we require that all of them are T for the result to be T. For OR only one input need be T for the returned value to be T.

How can we define a function which has an indefinite number of arguments? Let's not bother; rather, we'll give the new functions *lists* as arguments. Since a list can be as long as we like, this sidesteps the problem altogether. However, we must be careful to ensure that the structure of the argument list makes sense in the current context. In other words, it must be a 'flat list' such as that in Figure 7.

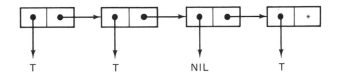

FIGURE 7. A flat list of TRUE or FALSE elements.

For the time being, we'll assume that it is somebody else's responsibility to check that this is so. There is a second constraint; both functions are meaningless unless applied to at least two Boolean values. Again, we'll defer consideration of this problem.

So we're just left with the problem of a recursive definition. Rule 1 states: "Solve the simplest case first". Here, the simplest case is the two-input condition to which we already have solutions. If there are two inputs, the tail of the tail of the list is NIL.

eq

The implication is clear. We have to test an atom to see if it's NIL. I have not introduced a predicate to do this yet, but one exists. It's called **eq** and takes two arguments, both of which should be atoms. If they are identical, it returns T, otherwise NIL. It isn't illegal to pass lists to **eq**, but NIL will always be returned, even when the lists are the same. Thus:

```
( setq x 'a )
( setq y 'a )
( eq x y )
```

returns T, but:

```
( setq x '( a b c ) )
( setq y '( a b c ) )
( eq x y )
```

returns NIL. The above is not intended as a *definition* of **eq**. It is far too imprecise. See Chapter 5 for more enlightenment.

Meanwhile Back at the Problem . . .

On to rule 2, which, you'll remember, requires us to decompose the general case into simpler versions of itself, ultimately arriving at the problem we've already solved. So, taking AND as an example, we could state the solution like this:

> If there are only two values in the list, AND them together.
> Otherwise, AND the head with the AND* of the tail.

Note that I've distinguished between the AND operation on two arguments, of which we already have a definition, and the AND* function, which operates on a list, and is the one we're trying to write.

Now it's easy:

```
( defun Al ( x )
    ( cond
        ( ( eq ( tail ( tail x ) ) NIL )
                    ( A ( head x ) ( head ( tail x ) ) )
        )
        ( T ( A ( head x ) ( Al ( tail x ) ) ) )
    )
)
```

I've replaced the AND* of the verbal definition with **Al** for 'AND on a list', but otherwise the two descriptions are virtually identical.

Keeping track of bracket matching becomes a shade tedious in this function. You might find it worthwhile writing the functions tail-of-tail and head-of-tail to reduce the problem a little. I'll leave it to you as an exercise, but remember that I mentioned earlier that such functions are usually already implemented, albeit under rather cryptic names.

null

Actually, my choice of **eq** in this example wasn't particularly sensible because there's a primitive, **null**, which returns T if its argument is the empty list. So the first line of the **cond** above could have read:

```
( ( null (tail_of_tail x) ) ( A (head x) (head_of_tail x) ) )
```

which is a good deal more straightforward and eliminates four brackets. It's very important to choose appropriate functions and primitives in a language which is as devoid of 'syntactic sugar' as Lisp is, because the alternative is to sink into a slough of impenetrable code. Equally, the smaller a function is the easier it is to debug.

AND and OR

I've already pointed out that primitives exist to evaluate Boolean functions. However, they do differ from the one built above in an important respect. They take indefinitely many arguments, rather than a single list. Thus you can write:

```
( and T T T NIL T T )
```

which would, of course, return NIL, or:

```
( or NIL NIL NIL T NIL T )
```

which would return T. Compare this with the action of the + primitive, which operates the same way. There are things to be said for both approaches. For instance, suppose we want to test for the condition that two variables, p and q, are both atoms and that r is an empty list. We might write:

```
( and (atom p) (atom q) (null r) )
```

To use my list equivalent here would be inconvenient, because we would have to create a list by repeatedly using **cons**. On the other hand, if we need to see if every terminal symbol of a complex list structure is T, the primitive function would be difficult to use. Wait a bit, though. The function **Al** is only defined for a flat list. It would be sensible to test its argument to confirm that it is correctly constructed before attempting to use the function.

flat

Let's write a function **flat** which returns T if its argument is a flat list and NIL otherwise. This time there are two fundamental conditions to consider:

1. If the list is null then it's flat.
2. If the argument is an atom then it's not flat, since it's not a list at all.

Otherwise, its head must be an atom and its tail must be flat.
In Lisp that becomes:

```
( defun flat ( x )
     ( cond
            ( (null x)   T )
            ( (atom x) NIL )
            ( (and (atom (head x) ) (flat (tail x) ) )     T )
            ( T     NIL )
     )
)
```

So we could use this function to warn that the function **Al** will have no meaning in a given set of circumstances, but it would be much nicer if **Al** could be made to work on any list, however complex its structure. One way of doing this would be to create a flat list from a list of arbitrary complexity and then use **Al** on the result. Let's examine this option in some detail. We'll call the new function **flatten**. Here's an approach which, as I'll explain in a moment, won't work:

```
( defun flatten ( x )
     ( cond
            ( (flat x)    x )
            (T (flatten(cons(flatten(head x))
                    (flatten (tail x) ))))
     )
)
```

The first part is easy; if it's a flat list then return it. Otherwise we want to flatten the head and the tail and **cons** the results. Unfortunately, the process of consing two lists is guaranteed to create a list which isn't flat since it adds a new head and tail at a higher level than the two sublists. No problem: we'll flatten that. If you try it out though, you'll quickly get a system message like 'stack overflow' which indicates that you've been somewhat profligate with memory. The difficulty is analogous to the 'endless loop' problem so often encountered in procedural languages. Every recursive call is building a list which is less flat than the head and tail of its argument because of the **cons**. So **flatten** is pulling in two directions at once. We appear to be in some difficulty, at least until we remember that there is one situation in which **cons** does not increase the complexity of the list structure, namely when an atom is consed with a list.

This gives a clue to a more productive approach. Suppose we write a function called **first** which returns the leftmost and deepest atom of a list and a second called **rest** which returns everything else. Then **flatten** becomes pretty straightforward:

```
( defun flatten ( x )
    ( cond
        ( (flat x)  x )
        ( T (cons (first x) ( flatten (rest x) ) ) ) )
    )
)
```

first

Let's think about the conditions we want. If the argument is an atom we'll return it. This is more a question of the definition of **first** than anything else. It would be equally legitimate to say that this situation is undefined and return NIL. The next simplest case is that the head is an atom , in which case, that's what we want to return. Otherwise we return the **first** of the head:

```
( defun first ( x )
    ( cond
        ( (atom x)   x )
        ( ( atom (head x) )    (head x) )
        ( T ( first (head x) ) ) )
    )
)
```

rest

This is slightly trickier, but not much. If the argument is an atom, there isn't a 'rest', so return NIL. If the head is an atom, we simply return the tail. Otherwise, we need the **rest** of the head together (i.e. consed) with the tail:

```
( defun rest ( x )
    ( cond
        ( (atom x) NIL )
        ( (atom (head x) )  (tail x) )
        ( T ( cons ( rest (head x) ) (tail x) ) )
    )
)
```

The Fly in the Ointment

Test these functions out. You should find that **first** and **rest** behave as
anticipated, but that, although **flatten** produces a flat list OK it is sometimes
sprinkled with spurious NILs. The problem is caused by Lisp's inability to
distinguish between the null list and the atom NIL. Thus when the list is
decomposed by **first**, sooner or later the (atom x) stage is reached with *x* being
NIL. **First** then returns NIL and this is consed on to the list returned by **flatten**.
One way out of this problem would be to write a function which removes NILs
from the list. Better yet, let's write **remove** which removes all incidences of the
atom *a* from the list *x*:

```
( defun remove ( a x )
     ( cond
        ( (null x) NIL )
        ( ( eq (head x) a ) ( remove a (tail x) ) )
        ( T ( cons (head x)
              ( remove a (tail x) ) ) )
     )
)
```

That's reasonably neat. If it's a null list return NIL. If the head is the target atom
return the tail with that atom removed. Otherwise, remove the atom from the
tail and cons the head on to the result.

Of course, this only works on a flat list; and if we use it to remove NILs we
have to be sure it isn't removing NILs that were there in the first place! This isn't
too serious a problem provided that the list consists of variables, though.

append and list

In fact, none of the above jiggery-pokery is actually necessary to write **flatten**.
There is a primitive called **append** which joins two lists (or a list and an atom) at
the same hierarchical level, so sidestepping the problem caused by **cons**. There is
another, **list**, which will form a list from an atom (so that, for instance, (b) is
formed from b). The difficulties now melt away:

```
( defun flatten ( x )
     ( cond
        ( (null x)   NIL )
        ( (atom x)   (list x) )
        ( T ( append ( flatten (head x) )
              ( flatten (tail x) ) ) )
     )
)
```

So if the list is null, we return NIL. If there is just an atom we form a list from it
and otherwise we flatten the head, flatten the tail and join them together.
Without the

```
( (atom x) (list x) )
```

the algorithm doesn't work when the head of a list is atomic because it tries to
take the head of an atom, which is illegal.

For instance, if x starts out as (a(b c d)), the first decomposition will attempt to flatten the head of a. However, if the line is present, the head of (a) is being flattened, which is fine.

Postscript

It may seem strange that I have devoted more than a little effort to the solution of the flattening problem when I could have dealt with it in a few lines if I had told you about **append** and **list** to begin with. I see it this way. The fundamental philosophy of Lisp is that complex and sophisticated systems can be written from a starting point at which the programmer is given very few tools, provided those tools are of the right type. In Chapter 2 I suggested that, of the list processing functions, only **car**, **cdr** and **cons** are actually necessary. While our discussion of **flatten** has not *proved* that to be the case, it has certainly provided useful evidence for it. Similarly, we've seen how an extremely restricted set of control constructs can be made to perform quite elaborate tasks. It may not have occurred to you just *how* tricky some of the functions in this chapter are because of the ease with which it has been possible to turn ideas into code. But try writing **first**, or **rest** or even **remove** in the procedural language of your choice in less than ten or fifteen lines. Admittedly, some extra work may be entailed because of the need to build a list structure which is inherent in Lisp, but bearing in mind the powerful constructs which Pascal or Ada or even modern versions of BASIC provide for the programmer, the relative economy of expression of the Lisp equivalents is quite striking.

Exercises 4

4.1 Write a function **element-p**(x list) that returns T if x is an element of the flat list *list*.

4.2 Write a function **fact**(n) to compute the factorial $n! = 1.2.3 \ldots n$ using the recursive formulas

$$0! = 1$$

$$n! = n(n-1)!$$

4.3 Write a function to compute binomial coefficients $c(n,r)$ using the recursive formulas

$$C(0,r) = 1$$

$$C(n,n) = 1$$

$$C(n,r) = C(n-1,r)+C(n-1,r-1)$$

Calculate $C(10,6)$.

4.4. Write a recursive function **sumsq** which evaluates the sum of squares of a flat list of integers.

4.5 Write a function **value** which, given a list of the form

```
(number1 + number2) or (number1 * number2)
```

calculates the appropriate sum or product.

4.6 Write a function **len** that returns the length of a flat list.

4.7 Using your answer to 4.5 recursively, write a function to evaluate any arithmetical formula such as

```
(((2 * 5) + 4) * ((3 + 1) * (6 + 7))).
```

Answers

4.1
```
( defun element-p(x list)
     ( cond
          ( (null list) NIL )
          ( (eq (head list) x)   T )
          ( T    (element-p x (tail list)) )
     )
)
```

4.2
```
( defun fact(n)
     ( cond
          ( (zerop n) 1 )
          ( T (* n (fact (- n 1))) )
     )
)
```

4.3
```
( defun bin(n r)
     ( cond
          ( (zerop n) 1)
          ( (= n r) 1)                    **
          ( T (+ (bin (- n 1) r)
             (bin (- n 1) (- r 1))))
     )
)
```

** For complicated reasons, **eq** might or might not work here, depending on the implementation. It is safer to use '=' for numeric equality tests.

4.4
```
( defun sumsq(x)
     ( cond
          ( (null x) NIL )
          ( (null(tail x))   (* (head x) (head x)))
          ( T (+ (* (head x) (head x))
                 (sumsq (tail x))))
     )
)
```

```
4.5      ( defun value(x)
              ( cond
                  ((eq(head(tail x)) '+)
                  (+ (head x)(head(tail(tail x)))))
                  ((eq(head(tail x)) '*)
                  (* (head x)(head(tail(tail x)))))
                  ( T NIL)
              )
         )

4.6      ( defun len(x)
              ( cond
                  ( (null x) 0)
                  ( T (+ 1 (len (tail x))))
              )
         )

4.7      ( defun revalue (x)
              ( cond
                  ((atom x) x)
                  ((eq(head(tail x)) '+)
                     (+(revalue(head x))
                         (revalue(head(tail(tail x))))))
                  ((eq(head(tail x)) '*)
                     (* (revalue(head x))
                         (revalue(head(tail(tail x))))))
                  (T NIL)
              )
         )
```

· 5 ·

A Look Back (and Forward)

"But wait a bit," the Oysters cried,
"Before we have our chat;
For some of us are out of breath,
And all of us are fat!"

Through the Looking-Glass

I could argue that, with the exception of the way LISP interfaces with the outside world, we have now met all its main features. It is possible, as I have already hinted, to build any function from **head**, **tail**, **append** and **cons**. However, the results would be pretty cryptic (especially if **head** and **tail** are replaced with the more conventional **car** and **cdr**.

So it's no surprise that builders of Lisp implementations have, over the years, provided users with more and more sophisticated and powerful primitives. Equally predictable is the fact that these new primitives differ between implementations in their actions and even their presence or absence.

By computing standards Lisp is a very old language; it has a heritage spanning nearly thirty years. So, in a sense, what is remarkable is not the range of dialects which have developed, but, rather, the fact that the examples I have presented so far will run on almost any of them.

Nevertheless, this is not an ideal situation. The computer science fraternity has, in recent years, become very concerned with the notion of *program portability*. A program is truly portable if it will run on any machine that is provided with a translator (interpreter or compiler) for the language in which the source code is written. The advantages of such portability are obvious. A great deal of programming time and effort is expended in making revisions to software to allow it to run on a range of different machines. While the goal of true portability has about it the attainability of the Holy Grail (for reasons that we shall examine later), any way of minimizing incompatibilities is obviously to be welcomed.

It was in this spirit that a large group of Lisp luminaries, working in different machine and implementation environments, joined forces around five years ago to define a common standard for the language. The result was Common Lisp, which can be thought of as a descendant of Maclisp and Zetalisp, with some features borrowed from Scheme and Interlisp. The language deliberately excludes constructs which might be difficult to implement on a particular machine, so the implementors are not tempted to omit or fudge specific features. On the other hand, features which might only be appropriate to a particular machine are also avoided, or, at least, made optional. The language definition is not exactly handed down in tablets of stone, but neither is it fluid. In other words, it is expected that the definition will change, for example by the addition of new primitives, but only after such additions have been examined very carefully. Since, in any environment, programmers will build their own functions thus adding to the 'local' language definition, it is possible to see all Common Lisp users as hothouses for new ideas and language extensions. This should avoid the problem, ever-present with a completely defined language like Pascal, that implementors are tempted to add new features which, they feel, users should not be without, thus neatly destroying the *point* of having a completely defined language.

So, for the remainder of this book, we shall concern ourselves with the Common Lisp philosophy. It is a huge language and it would be inappropriate in an introductory text such as this to deal exhaustively with all its features. What I shall aim to do is to look at all the most popular constructs and give you the confidence to research others for yourself from your system manuals.

Variables: a Sense of Place

While in reflective mood I want to examine in more detail the nature of Lisp variables. Thus far, I have used them without comment as though they were like BASIC or Pascal variables and that has suited my purpose well enough. However,there are a number of differences that I wish to explore.

First, write the following sequence to the interpreter:

```
( setq x 3 )
( setq x 'a )
( setq x '(( a b )( c d e )) )
```

You get the responses:

> 3
> A

and ((A B)(C D E)) respectively. In other words, the interpreter has happily assigned first a number, then a character and finally a list to the same variable. In most languages, even those that do not force you to specify the type of a variable before you use it, we would have been met with an error message as soon as we tried to 'retype' *x* from a number to a character.

It's useful to think about the actions an interpreter (or compiler) must take in response to such assignments. Let's suppose a BASIC interpreter meets:

> 20 x = 3

It may respond by assigning the name *x* to a byte (or two) and allocating the following 16 bits to the integer 3. The following assignment:

> 30 x = "A"

assuming its syntax were legal, would be achievable because the character code for 'A' would fit in 16 bits. However, an attempt to print the contents of *x* could yield nothing but confusion because the system would be unable to distinguish between an integer and a numeric code representing a character.

Assuming that our hypothetical interpreter can handle lists at all, it's clear that it cannot do so in a 16-bit field. So Lisp must be employing a different technique for assigning variables to objects. The obvious alternative is to see the variable name as a pointer to the Lisp object being assigned. Now reassignment merely means a change of pointer value.

While this should be transparent to the user, it *can* lead to subtle traps for the unwary. For instance, the **eq** predicate may be implemented by examining whether the pointers to the two arguments are identical; that is, it asks not "are the objects equivalent?", but "are they the same object?" (see Figure 8).

FIGURE 8. Some **eqs** are more equal than others: (a) (eq x y) is T; (b) (eq x y) is NIL.

Normally the distinction is academic because the interpreter does not need to hold several copies of the same object—in fact, it would be inefficient to do so because more memory than necessary would be allocated. However, it *can* happen, with potentially confusing results.

It is important to see a variable name as providing 'place' information about the object to which it refers, because we can then view it as a special case of a general class of 'placing' attributes, as we shall see later.

Variable Scope

Now try something else:

```
( setq x 20 )
( defun test ( x )
        ( + x 6 )
)
```

Then write:

```
( test 10 )
```

The interpreter responds with 16 as you'd expect. Now try:

```
( + x )
```

You'll see:

```
20
```

(Note that + doesn't need two arguments.)

I've deliberately given *x* two distinct meanings. First, it's a variable, assigned the value 20. Second, it's an argument of the function **test**. Passing 10 to the function has had no effect on the originally assigned value, which we can see is still 20. Evidently, Lisp is happy to distinguish between the two *x*'s.

One way of describing what is happening here is to say that the *scope* of a variable (i.e. the region in which it has a meaning) is limited according to certain rules. Let's experiment a little more before attempting an analysis. Type:

```
( defun test2 ( y )
        ( + y 2 )
)
```

Now

```
( test2 3 )
```

yields 5, as you'd expect, but:

```
( + y )
```

gives an error message (probably 'Unbound symbol').

So in the first example, *x* reverted to its original meaning once the function **test** had been left and in the second case *y* has a meaning only within **test2**.

Variable Binding

We say that a function definition *binds* its arguments, so that *y* is bound in **test2** because it is an argument (indeed *the* argument) of **test2**. However, what *y* is bound *to* changes with each invocation of the function. In the example above, *y* is bound to 3. (test2 7) would bind *y* to 7, and so on.

Now the meaning of the error message is clearer. Because the interpreter is being asked to evaluate (+ y 2) outside the function, it is also outside the scope of y and so the variable is not bound.

Free Variables

Now consider this :

```
( setq a 6 )
( defun inca ( x )
      ( + x a )
)
( inca 4 )
```

gives 10, as you'd expect. Clearly, *a* is not bound in **inca**, but neither is any error signalled. *a* is said to be a *free* variable. More precisely, *a* is free in **inca**. It must be bound *somewhere* or an error would have resulted. We can think of it as bound in the *global environment* because it is universally available.

Note incidentally that the function names (**test**, **inca** etc.) themselves are bound, again globally, because they are arguments to **defun**.

Lexical Scoping

So far, we have seen functions as being completely independent of one another. However, it's quite possible to include one function definition inside another. For example, suppose that we require a function that will return a value one closer to zero then its argument. So if it is passed 7 it returns 6 and if it is passed −3 it returns −2. The following will do, assuming that we already have the functions **dec** and **inc** previously defined:

```
( defun tozero ( x )
          ( cond
                    ( ( > x 0 ) ( dec x ) )
                    ( (zerop x)    x    )
                    (    T         ( inc x ) ) )
          )
)
```

['>' is a primitive predicate which returns T if its arguments, which must be numbers, are in descending order. As we've seen in Exercises 4, = also exists, and so do <,<= and >=.] If **inc** and **dec** are not available they can be defined within **tozero**:

```
( defun tozero ( x )
            ( defun inc ( x ) ( + x 1 ) )
            ( defun dec ( x ) ( - x 1 ) )
        ( cond
                    ( ( > x 0 ) ( dec x ) )
                    ( (zerop x)      x )
                    ( T            ( inc x ) )
          )
)
```

This version of the function is not wrong, but it does illustrate an interesting anomaly. Since *x* is bound in **tozero** any function defined in **tozero** knows the value *x* is bound to and so need not be passed this value. So I can rewrite **tozero** again :

```
( defun tozero ( x )
        ( defun inc ( ) ( + x 1 ) )
        ( defun dec ( ) ( - x 1 ) )
     ( cond
               ( ( > x 0 ) ( dec ) )
               ( (zerop x)       x )
               (    T        ( inc ) )
        )
)
```

Now **inc** and **dec** have no arguments, so their argument lists are empty. The two functions are invoked by creating a list with the function name in it, as in (dec). This is the first time I have mentioned the idea of a function with no arguments, but it's not uncommon and you may already have discovered one yourself, namely (exit). If not, you've been stuck in the Lisp system for the last five chapters.

We say that *x* is *lexically scoped* because any occurrence of the variable is referred back to its most recent binding, in this case provided by the definition of **tozero**. Perhaps a more prosaic way of thinking about it would be to say that the binding is derived from the context (hence lexical). The term *static binding* is sometimes used equivalently.

A Software Engineering Problem

Suppose that you loaded the old version of **inc** and **dec** and subsequently entered the definition of **tozero** above. If you then write:

```
( inc 7 )
```

you'll be greeted with an error message, probably indicating that there are too many arguments to the function. This is none too surprising because **defun** has generated a global rebinding of inc, destroying the old definition. Now, inc is unusable outside **tozero**; if you write:

```
( inc)
```

you'll be told that *x* is unbound. Of course it is. We're outside **tozero** and therefore outside the scope of *x*.

While all this might not create too many problems if a single programmer were responsible for all the code in a project, it's easy to imagine the chaos that could be caused if twenty or thirty programmers, as is commonly the case, were building a system. There might be multiple definitions of the same function, different functions with the same name and varying numbers of arguments and so on. And there's more . . .

setq

A similar problem arises with variable assignment. Try:

```
( defun test ( )
        ( setq x 1 )
)
```

Now you might expect *x* to be local to **test**. But if you invoke **test** and then use *x*, like this, say

```
( test )
( + x )
```

you will not get the 'unbound symbol' message. Lisp will respond happily that *x* is 1. Again, a little careful thought explains this. *x* is bound in the definition of **setq** which is global. Hence *x* is global even though it is referenced only inside a function.

For the moment, I do not wish to offer a solution to these problems; I am content merely to observe that they exist and that we shall have to confront them sooner or later. This is an application of the Jones–Maynard–Stewart first law of computing: Never put off till tomorrow what you can put off till the day after.

System Variables

There are various global variables that are set by the system and which can be accessed and modified by the user. These all have the form *variable-name*. The double asterisk notation is used to reduce the possibility of confusion with user defined variables. Notice also that a minus sign is used as a separator, rather than an underscore. Although the use of the underscore is not illegal in Common Lisp, it is frowned upon, because it is reserved in the language definition for future system use. Consequently, a program written now using underscores could not be guaranteed to work on subsequent Common Lisp interpreters although it would be fine at the moment.

Examples of system variables are:

print-base
This defines the radix in which integers are output. It is initialized to 10 but can be reset to any value from 2 to 36. So:

```
( setq *print-base* 16 )
( setq x 30 )
```

will respond with 1E because all output is now in hexadecimal.

print-case
You will have noticed that Lisp outputs everything in uppercase however the data were entered. This can be altered by changing *print-case*. It can be :upcase (the initial value), :downcase or :capitalize. Thus:

```
( setq *print-case* :downcase)
```

will set all output to lower case. Note, but do not for the time being worry about, the colon notation.

Exercises 5

These exercises are not related to the contents of this chapter, but are merely intended to jog your memory and implant more firmly what we have covered so far.

5.1 Write a function **tsil** which reverses a flat list.

5.2 Use **tsil** to write a function **last** which picks out the last element of a flat list.

5.3 Write a function **butlast** which returns everything except the last element of a flat list.

5.4 A Fibonacci series consists of the sum

$$1 + 1 + 2 + 3 + 5 + 8 + 13 + \ldots$$

in which each term is the sum of the previous two. Write the function **fibterm**(n) which returns the nth term.

5.5 Using **fibterm**, write the function **fibsum** to evaluate the sum of n terms.

Answers

```
5.1     ( defun tsil(x)
             ( cond
                  ( (null x) NIL )
                  ( T (append (tsil (tail x))
                             (list (head x))))
             )
        )

5.2     ( defun last(x)
             (head (tsil x))
        )

5.3     ( defun butlast(x)
             ( head (tail (tsil x)))
        )

5.4     ( defun fibterm(n)
             ( cond
                  ( (zerop n)  0 )
                  ( (= n 1) 1 )
                  ( T (+ fibterm (dec n))
                            (fibterm (- n 2))))
             )
        )

5.5     ( defun fibsum(n)
             ( cond
                  ( (zerop n)  0 )
                  ( T (+ (fibterm n) (fibsum (dec n))))
             )
        )
```

· 6 ·

Sets and Lists

Alice thought to herself "Thirty times three makes ninety. I wonder if any one's counting?"

Through the Looking-Glass

Having suggested in Chapter 5 that you can do pretty much anything with the tools we already have, now would be a good time to demonstrate it. We'll build a group of functions that have applications in set theory. I've chosen this example partly because there is such a convenient link between a set and a list (or, at any rate, a flat list). To some extent, we are reinventing the wheel, in that several of these functions are already present in Common Lisp, but it's still a useful exercise to see how they might be written. For our purposes, it will be sensible to define a set as a flat list with non-repeating elements. So (A B C D) is a set, but (A B C B D) is not.

Sets of Numbers

We'll start by writing some functions that create specific sets which we can then use for testing the remaining functions. First, then, a function called **evens** that returns a list of the even integers up to its argument (excluding zero):

```
(defun evens(max)
     (cond
          ( (= max 2)   '(2) )
          ( T    (cons max (evens (- max 2)))))
     )
)
```

This is pretty straightforward. If the maximum value in the list is to be 2, then return the list (2). Otherwise return the **cons** of max with the list of even numbers up to max -2. Of course, since the last value to be consed on to the list will always be the highest, the set will appear in descending order, but this is OK since we made no stipulation about the order of the elements of a set in the definition. It's now obvious that it would be easy to write a more general function that gives all multiples of any number up to a given maximum:

```
(defun multiples(number max)
     (cond
          ( (= max number)    (list number) )
          ( T (cons max (multiples number
                              (- max number)))))
     )
)
```

We can easily see that this is just a more general case of **evens** by substituting 2 for *number* and comparing the two functions. Notice, though, the use of the **list** primitive to form a list from an atom.

The Set Functions

We already have one useful set function in our armoury from Chapter 4—**element-p** (see Exercise 4.1). However, this will only test for the presence of an atom in a list *at least* once, so we'll need a precursor that confirms that the list is indeed a set. The trivial case is the empty set, which is certainly legal, and we return T. Otherwise, we'll have to examine the head of the list to see if it's an element of the tail of the list. If it is, the list is not a set; there's a repeated element, and NIL is returned:

```
(defun set-p(list)
     (cond
          ( (null list)     T)
          ( (element-p (head list)   (tail list))   NIL)
```

But that still leaves us with the 'catch-all' condition. It's easy! If the head isn't in the tail, then the list is a set if the tail itself is a set:

```
          (T (set-p (tail list) ) )
     )
)
```

It's interesting to compare this example with its equivalent in a procedural language. You would have to write a piece of code that compared the first element of the list with each of the others, then the second with all except the first, then the third with all except the first and second, and so on. That will lead to nested iterations and fairly careful thought. In Lisp, once the function *definition* has been arrived at, the code almost writes itself.

Intersection

Now let's try the intersection of two sets. This is the set containing only those elements that are common to the two argument sets. So if set1 is (A B C D E) and set2 is (C E F G H), (I set1 set2) should return (C E). We'll build the definition from the trivial case up, as usual.

1. If set2 is empty, the intersection is empty.
2. If the head of set2 is an element of set1, the intersection is the **cons** of this atom with the intersection of set1 and the tail of set2.
3. Otherwise, it's the intersection of set1 with the tail of set2.

For instance, if set1 is (A B C D) and set2 is (A C E), rule 2 applies and the intersection is:

```
(cons 'A (I '(A B C D) '(C E)))
```

It can be useful to set up little examples like this to convince yourself that a definition really works. Don't be tempted to 'dry run' a function in the way you might with a procedural language, though. Brain-fade sets in very quickly and, in any case, the exercise isn't really useful. The more you use *definition* rather than *action* as the basis for writing Lisp functions, the easier it becomes. Here's the final code:

```
( defun I (set1 set2)
    ( cond
          ( (null set2) NIL )
          ( (element-p (head set2) set 1)
              (cons (head set2) (I set1 (tail set2))) )
          ( T (I set1 (tail set2)) )
    )
)
```

We can test the function using **multiples**, like this, for instance:

```
(I (multiples 5 30) (multiples 3 42) )
```

which should return the set (30 15), or, in other words, multiples of 15.

disjoint-p

Now we'll write the function **disjoint-p** which returns T only if its arguments contain no common elements:

```
(defun disjoint-p (set1 set2)
     (cond
          ( (null (I set1 set2))  T)
          ( T NIL )
     )
)
```

That's simple enough, but there's an even easier alternative. To write it you need to know that Lisp regards anything that is not NIL as T for the purposes of a predicate. Thus it is legitimate to write:

```
(cond
       (x    T)
          :
          :
```

even if x is known to be a list such as (A B C). If it is, T will be returned. Only if x is the empty list will the **cond** examine the next predicate/expression pair. Given this hint, can you write a simplified **disjoint-p**?

Subsets

Next we'll write the **subset** function, which will return T only if set2 is completely contained within set1. It needs no detailed analysis:

```
(defun C(set1 set2)
     (cond
          ( (equal set2 (I set1 set2))     T)
          ( T    NIL )
     )
)
```

Notice the use of **equal** rather than **eq** to compare lists. I shall have more to say on this later, but, for the moment, simply regard **equal** as a more generally applicable predicate than **eq**.

Incidentally, this function, like **disjoint-p**, can be more simply written. Can you see how?

You can run tests such as:

```
(C (multiples 4 40) (multiples 8 40) )        and:
(C (multiples 5 20) (multiples 2 20) )
```

Complement

The complement of a set depends on the definition of the universe within which we are currently operating. For example, if the universe is all positive integers up to 100, or (multiples 1 100) the complement of 'all even numbers up to 100' is 'all odd numbers up to 100'. We have, in fact, already written one complement function (~), which provided the complement of T or NIL in a universe consisting just of (T NIL). I shall reuse this function name here, since there is a Common Lisp primitive **not** that does the job of our previous function and this is clearly a more general case of the same thing. The rules are:

1. if the universe is empty the complement of any set is empty
2. if the head of the universe is an element of the set then the complement is the same as the complement of the set in the tail of the universe.
3. Otherwise the complement is the **cons** of the head of the universe with the complement of the set in the tail of the universe.

This gives us:

```
(defun ~(universe set)
     (cond
            ( (null universe)      NIL )
            ( (element-p (head universe) set)
                    (~ (tail universe)   set) )
            (T (cons (head universe)
                    (~ (tail universe) set)))
     )
)
```

This function looks a little strange, partly because of the test for a null universe. It is clear only when you realize that the rest of the definition *must* decompose the universe rather than the set, so that we need a null universe to terminate the recursion. As usual, a few examples will convince you of the validity of the definition. Try, for instance, the complement of (5 3 1) in the universe (multiples 1 5).

The universe is not null and the head of the universe is an element of the set, so rule 2 applies:

```
(~ '(4 3 2 1) '(5 3 1))
```

If this is presented to the function, rule 3 applies, since the head of the universe (now 4) does not appear in the set:

```
( cons 4 (~ '(3 2 1) '(5 3 1)))
```

and we can see how the complement is being built.

Union

The union of two sets consists of the set containing all elements that appear in at least one of them. Clearly, we can't just *append* the two sets, because that would include their intersection twice. However, we *can* append set1 excluding the intersection with set2. Now set1 excluding the intersection is the complement of the intersection of set1 and set2 in the universe set1. That gives us:

```
(defun U(set1 set2)
     (append (~ set1 (I set1 set2)) set2)
)
```

which you can test with things like:

> (U (multiples 2 20) (multiples 3 21))

in which 6, 12 and 18 should appear only once.

Exercises 6

To illustrate the power of the ideas in this chapter, the following exercises apply our suite of set-theoretic functions to some questions in number theory. In number theory, a set that consists of all multiples (positive, negative or zero) of a given integer is called an *ideal*. The integer used to produce the multiples is called the *generator* of the ideal. For example the ideal with generator 5 is the set (. . . . −15 −10 −5 0 5 10 15 . . .). The set-theoretic properties of ideals are closely related to the prime factorization of integers. The exercises below explore some of the basic properties of ideals in an 'experimental mathematics' setting. In the absence of infinite memory (and time!) we arbitrarily restrict the integers involved to the range 1–100.

6.1 The function **multiples** (*number max*) defined earlier has an awkward feature: it only works if *max* is an exact multiple of *number*. (Try (multiples 3 7)!). Modify it to work with any positive integer arguments. Use the result to define the function **ideal** (*generator*) which returns the set of all multiples of *generator* that lie in the range 1–100.

   (You may want to use the primitive **mod**. (mod x y) returns the remainder of *x/y*.)

6.2 Write a function **minimum** (*set*) which returns NIL if *set* is null and the smallest member of the set otherwise. (Remember that we only need to consider positive integers.) Use this to define a function **ideal-p** (*set*) which returns T if *set* is an ideal (under the 1–100 restriction) and NIL otherwise.

6.3 Modify **ideal-p** to define the function **generator** (*set*) which returns the generator of *set* if *set* is an ideal and NIL if not.

6.4 Is the union of two ideals also an ideal? Write a function **uideal-p** (*m n*) to investigate this. It should return T if the union of (ideal m) and (ideal n) is an ideal, NIL otherwise.

6.5 Write an analogous function **iideal-p** (*m n*) to test whether the intersection of (ideal m) and (ideal n) is an ideal. Improve on your answer to 6.4 by making **iideal** return the generator when the intersection is an ideal.

6.6 Use the answer to 6.5 to calculate:

```
(ideal 5) n (ideal 7)
(ideal 4) n (ideal 5)
(ideal 6) n (ideal 15)
(ideal 6) n (ideal 9)
```

Formulate a conjecture along the lines

```
(ideal m) n (ideal n) = (ideal r)
```

6.7 It is a theorem that (ideal m) is a subset of (ideal n) if and only if *n* divides *m* exactly. Write a function subset-p(*m n*) to test this. It should return T if (ideal m) is a subset of (ideal n) and NIL otherwise. Test it with *m* = 6, *n* = 3 and *m* = 3, *n* = 6, when it should return T, NIL respectively.

Answers

6.1   (defun multi(number max)
            (cond
                    ((< max number) NIL)
                    ((= 0 (mod max number))
                            (multiples number max))
                    (T (multi number (- max 1)))
)
)

6.2   (defun minimum(set)
            (cond
                    ((null set) NIL)
                    ((null (tail set))   (head set))
                    ((< (head set)
                        (minimum (tail set)))   (head set))
                    (T (minimum (tail set)))
)
)
        (defun ideal-p(set)
            (cond
                    ((equal (ideal (minimum set)) set) T)
                    (T NIL)
)
)

6.3   (defun generator(set)
            (cond
                    ((equal (ideal (minimum set)) set)
                                (minimum set))
                    (T NIL)
)
)

6.4   (defun uideal-p(m n)
            (ideal-p (U (ideal m) (ideal n)))
)

6.5   (defun iideal-p(m n)
            (generator (I (ideal m) (ideal n)))
)

6.6   (ideal 5) n (ideal 7) = (ideal 35)
        (ideal 4) n (ideal 5) = (ideal 20)

which might suggest that (ideal m) n (ideal n) = (ideal mn). However,

        (ideal 6) n (ideal 15) = (ideal 30)
        (ideal 6) n (ideal 9) = (ideal 18)

and the correct statement is

        (ideal m) n (ideal n) = (ideal (lcm m n))

where (lcm m n) is the lowest common multiple of m and n.

6.7   (defun subset-p(m n)
            (C(ideal n) (ideal m))
)

· 7 ·

Input

The last time she saw them, they were trying to put the Dormouse into the teapot.

Alice's Adventures in Wonderland

So far I have been less than forthcoming about how to make Lisp communicate with the outside world. This hasn't been too much of a problem so far, because of Lisp's rather voluble nature. That is, it returns the result of a function to us as soon as it has completed. However, we will only find out the result of the outermost function and the layout will leave much to be desired.

Also, at the moment we have no way at all of inputting data; we have had to resort to assignments using **setq**. Let's remedy the latter problem first.

read

There are a number of primitive functions to enable inputs to be performed. The most general is **read**. To see it operating at its simplest, type:

```
(read)
```

Lisp is now waiting for some input. Type '3'. The screen display is now:

    `(read)3`

since no formatting instructions have been supplied. Now hit RETURN. The screen display becomes:

    `(read)3`   (assuming your implementation does not
    `3`   need a RETURN after the ')')

indicating that **read** has accepted the '3' and returned it.

So it should be possible to add two input numbers by:

    `( + (read) (read) )`

Try this, and enter two numbers, following each by *any* white-space character such as RETURN, SPACE or TAB. You'll find it works as predicted. In fact, you can have indefinitely many white-space symbols between or preceding the two numbers. **read** ignores all of them except those immediately following the numbers, which it treats as delimiters. **read** is happy to handle Lisp objects other than numbers. For instance :

    `(read)( ( A B ) ( C D E ( F G ) ) )`

will return:

    `( ( A B ) ( C D E ( F G ) ) )`

Clearly, there are spaces here which are not being seen as delimiters, but **read** has no problem with this because the brackets provide the cue that a list is being entered. If we want to preserve white-space characters there is another function to do the job:

read-line

Try:

    `(read-line) ab cd efg`

followed by RETURN. The system responds:

    `" ab cd efg"`
    `NIL`

Ignore the 'NIL' for the time being. The important point is that **read-line** has placed double quote marks around the string, a technique familiar to programmers in many languages. So **read** should accept the same string delimited by double quotes:

    `(read) " ab cd efg"`

and you'll see that it does.

Single Characters

A further function, **read-char** will accept a single character without the need for a delimiter.

Try:

>   (read-char)d

Lisp responds:

>   #\d

The symbols '#\' are called an *escape sequence* and are used to denote that d is the single character 'd' and not (for instance) the atom 'D'. Non-printing characters are escaped in the same way. For instance if you hit the space bar in response to a **read-char**, it will return:

>   #\SPACE

Other common values are:

>   #\NEWLINE
>   #\TAB
>   #\PAGE   (in response to CTRL-L)

Note also that :

>   (read-char)6

will return:

>   #\6   (the *character* code whose representation is 6)

but:

>   (read)6

will return:

>   6   (the *number* 6)

More About

The # symbol is used to introduce other kinds of sequence. In particular #b indicates a binary number, #x a hexadecimal number and #0 an octal number. So, for instance :

>   (read)#x1a4

will elicit the response:

>   420   (1 * 256 + 10 * 16 + 4)

For other arithmetic bases, the form *#nrdddd* is used, where *n* is the required base and *dddd* represents the digits in that base. Thus:

>   (read)#3r121

yields:

>   16   (1 * 9 + 2 * 3 + 1)

There are other uses for # which I shall temporarily defer.

Yes or No Responses

Very commonly, we want to write a piece of code in which the user's response to a single yes/no question determines the program's action. A classic example would give a message such as "Do you really want to destroy all your files?" and request a single input character, 'y' or 'n'. Clearly, a function to do this job could be built from **read-char** and, indeed, it already has been. It has the form:

```
( y-or-n-p string )
```

The string provides a prompt on the screen and **y-or-n-p** returns T if the user enters 'y' or 'Y', NIL if the user enters 'n' or 'N' and repeats the question otherwise. So:

```
( y-or-n-p "Carry on ?" )
```

will generate:

```
Carry on ?
Enter Y or N :
```

Using the read Primitives

Let's tie these ideas together in a (very) simple example. Suppose we wish to create a list representing a telephone directory. Its form is to be:

```
(ZOE 8371 HARRY 9142 JIM 1248 JOE 1617 ALICE 3694)
```

indicating that Zoe's number is 8371, Jim's is 1248 etc.

We'll define three functions, which will operate on a global list called telnum:

init   will initialize the list.
add   will add a single entry consisting of a NAME, NUMBER pair to the list.
build   will build the list by repeatedly calling **add**.

init is easy:

```
( defun init ( )
        ( setq telnum NIL )
)
```

add requires a little thought; first we want to read a name and **cons** it with telnum:

```
( cons ( read ) telnum )
```

Then we need to read the telephone number and **cons** that on to the list:

```
( cons ( read ) ( cons ( read ) telnum ) )
```

Finally the result must be assigned to telnum:

```
( defun add ( )
    ( setq telnum ( cons (read )
                         ( cons (read ) telnum ) ) )
  )
```

build performs an add, then asks if there are any more additions, calling **build** again if there are. Otherwise it returns T (for no particularly good reason):

```
( defun build ( )
        ( add )
        ( cond
                ( ( y-or-n-p "Any more?") (  build ) )
                (    T    T )
        )
)
```

This works OK but it's hardly user friendly. There are no prompts to indicate what input data are required and there's no spacing at all. You get a display like:

```
(build)alice 3694
Any more ?
Enter Y or N : yjoe 1617
Any more ?
Enter Y or N : yjim 1248
```

and so on.
    You can check that the list has been formed correctly with:

```
(list telnum)
```

which will, of course, return a list with an extra pair of brackets. Notice that the list is formed from right to left because each call to **add** adds a new head to it. However, the NAME, NUMBER pairs appear in the order they are entered because the **read** calls in **add** are evaluated as they are encountered, *not* deepest level first.
    Our next problem is to make things *look* better . . .

Exercises 7

7.1 Write a function to create a list of arbitrary length from a series of inputs of positive integers, using 0 as a delimiter.
7.2 Modify your answer to 7.1 to allow the user to specify his own delimiter.

Answers

```
7.1    (setq x NIL )
       ( defun getlist()
            ( setq temp (read) )
            ( cond
                 ( (= temp 0)  T )
                 ( .T    (concat) )
            )
       )
       ( defun concat()
            ( setq x (cons temp x) )
            (getlist)
       )
```

(There is a neater way of doing this but we need a function that hasn't been described yet. Anyway, it's an interesting example of recursion in which each of two functions calls the other.)

7.2
```
(setq x NIL)
( defun getlist(delim)
      ( setq temp (read) )
      ( cond
            ( (= temp delim)  T )
            ( T (concat delim) )
      )
)
```

And **concat** has to change . . .

```
( defun concat(delim)
      ( setq x (cons temp x) )
      (getlist delim)
)
```

· 8 ·

Output

"I see you're admiring my little box," the Knight said in a friendly tone. "It's my own invention—to keep clothes and sandwiches in. You see I carry it upside-down, so that the rain can't get in."

"But the things can get out," Alice gently remarked. "Do you know the lid's open?"

Through the Looking-Glass

There is a range of functions that Common Lisp provides for talking to the outside world. The most generally useful is **format**, so we'll discuss that first.

format

In its full glory, **format** is a function of mind-blowing sophistication and power. Some of its features are so complicated that it's difficult to think of uses for them. So I'm going to restrict our discussions to a kind of vanilla-flavoured version of the function. For starters, try this:

```
(format T "Some output")
```

The screen appearance is:

```
(format T "Some output")Some output
NIL
```

In other words the function has printed the message 'Some output' and then returned NIL. Note the presence of T as the first argument to format (it *must* be there) but do not worry about it for the time being.

The Control String

The second argument is called a *control string*. In the above example it doesn't seem to be controlling much. In fact, the contents of the control string are always printed out *unless* a tilde (~) appears in it. The tilde acts as an introducer to a control section of the string. For example, the form ~5% will output five new lines. So:

```
(format T "This ~2% is on ~3% several ~4% lines")
```

will output:

```
This
  is on

  several


  lines
```

Printing Values

We can include the value of a variable in the output by entering ~A in the control string. Clearly, we must also provide **format** with the name of the variable whose value is to be printed. For instance:

```
(format T "There are ~A characters in the text" c)
```

If the value of *c* is 318, this would output:

```
There are 318 characters in the text
```

It is also possible to assign a specific quantity of space to the value as in:

```
(format T "There are ~8A characters in the text" c)
```

This allocates 8 character positions to the value 318 so we get:

```
There are 318     characters in the text
```

Notice that the value is left-justified in its field. It is possible to force **format** to right-justify its arguments by preceding the 'A' with an '@' symbol:

```
(format T "There are ~8@A characters in the text" c)
```

would give:

```
There are      318 characters in the text
```

There may be multiple arguments and a corresponding number of entries in the control string. In such cases the arguments match, left to right, with the corresponding entries in the control string. Thus in:

```
(format T "There are ~5@A words and ~9A characters
in the text" w c)
```

the ~5@A is matched with *w* and the ~9A is matched with *c* giving a display like:

```
There are  68 words and 318     characters
in the text
```

Format Directives

The sequences introduced with a tilde are called format directives and they have, in general, a more complex form than I have so far indicated. The '*A*' directive has four parameters all of which have default values, so that in simple cases, as we've seen, they need not be quoted at all. The full form is:

```
~w,i,m,pA
```

w is the minimum field width. There are at least *m* pad characters, *p*, following the printed value. If this does not use up *w* characters, *i* pad characters are inserted repeatedly until the field is at least *w* characters wide. The default value of *p* is #\SPACE (as you can deduce from the above examples), those for *w* and *m* are zero and *i* is 1. If you want to alter only some of the parameters you can omit those to which the defaults still apply, but it's safer and simpler to specify the lot since they are position dependent.

Try experimenting to see the effects; always use printing pad characters to make the results easy to analyse. For example:

```
(setq x 2999)
(format T "~12,4,0,'*A" x)
```

will give:

```
2999********
```

taking up exactly 12 characters because 12 is divisible by four, but:

```
(format T "~6,4,0,'=A" x)
```

outputs:

```
2999====
```

because only four characters are occupied by the value and so a further four pad characters are added before the total of six is reached. Again:

```
(format T "~0,0,10,'xA" x)
```

displays:

```
2999xxxxxxxxxx
```

because I have specified a minimum of 10 pad characters.

Using Arguments as Parameters

Any of the parameters of a format directive can be replaced by the letter V. At execution time **format** replaces this with the next value from the argument list. For instance:

```
(format T "~%~0,0,V,'-A" x "test" )
```

will output 2999 minus signs following 'test' because the minimum number of pad characters is set to 2999.

Tabs

The format directive $\sim n, s$T allows you to tabulate output. The value of n specifies the column at which the cursor is to be placed. The value of s gives the number of columns to skip if the cursor is already past the specified position. (In fact s columns will be repeatedly added to the column value until it is past the cursor position.) In practice, something has probably gone wrong with the layout anyway if the value of s comes into play, so it's convenient to set it to 1. Since that's its default value it can be omitted completely. So:

```
(format T "~40T~A" x)
```

will output 2999 starting in column 40.

In fact, if you're printing numbers, it's more likely that you want them right-justified in their columns, so a more probable specification would be:

```
(format T "~40T~6@A" x)
```

which would leave spaces in columns 40 and 41, and the digits of the number in columns 42 to 45.

A combination of T and V can be made to produce some very fancy effects.

Other Output Functions

There are a number of simpler functions than **format**, some of which are briefly described below.

(terpri)   simply outputs a new-line character and returns NIL.

(write-char)   outputs the single character *c* and returns *c*.

(print x)   outputs a new-line character followed by the value of *x*, which is any Lisp object, and then returns *x*. So if you use this at the top level of the intepreter *x* will appear twice.

(write-string s b e)   outputs the string *s*. The other arguments *b* and *e* are optional and define the beginning and end of the substring to be output. For example:

```
(write-string "0123467" 2 5)
```

will output:

```
234
```

The string is counted from character zero and the last character output is the one *before* the value of *e*.

(unread-char c)   In a sense, this isn't an output function at all. It takes the last character input and puts it back where it came from. It's probably not clear why it would be useful but we will come across it later.

The Telephone Index Again

Now we can return to the telephone index problem of Chapter 7 and make the program's interaction with the user somewhat less brusque:

```
(defun init ( )
      (format T "~5%Telephone index being initialized" )
      (setq tel-index NIL )
)
(defun add ( )
  (format T "~2%New entry;enter name then number~%" )
  (setq tel-index(cons(read) (cons(read) tel-index ) ) )
)
```

build remains unchanged.

The read–eval–print Loop

The *read* and *print* functions discussed in the last two chapters are not merely available to the user; they are used by the interpreter *in a loop* to accept the user's code and display results. In between, there must clearly be something to act upon, or *evaluate* the input code or data. This task is performed by a function called **eval** which is, of course, also available to the user.

eval will evaluate anything in sight. So where, for instance, I have suggested that you confirm the value of a variable with (+ x) or (list tel-index) it would actually have been simpler just to type *x* or *tel-index*. Thus if you write:

```
(setq x 'xvalue )
(setq y 'x )
```

Lisp will tell you that *y* is the atom X. However if you type:

```
(eval y )
```

you'll get the response:

```
XVALUE
```

because Lisp has determined that *y* is *x* and that *x* has the value XVALUE. An attempt to:

```
(eval xvalue )
```

will lead, fairly obviously, to an 'unbound symbol' message. However, evaluating a constant *is* legal. The constant is returned unaltered. So:

```
(eval 7)        returns 7
(eval "test")  returns "test"
```

The Program–Data Distinction

In most languages, program and data are distinct entities. It is not possible to alter or add to an existing program in, say, FORTRAN, by inputting some data for this purpose at run time. In Lisp, though, the **eval** function allows us to do exactly that. Try:

```
(eval (read) )
```

The system will hang up, waiting for the input. Now enter:

```
(defun inc ( x ) ( + x 1) )
```

Lisp returns:

```
INC
```

just as if the definition had taken place at the top level of the interpreter; **inc** has been added to the available functions. This isn't too surprising since we're merely doing explicitly what the interpreter would do anyway, but it does add an extra level of flexibility to the features of the language. We shall exploit this facility later, when we come to write an interpreter.

Exercises 8

8.1 Write a function which takes a list of dates, of the shape

```
( (25 March 1962) (4 July 1776) (7 May 1988) ..)
```

and writes it as a table with tabs at 0, 10 and 20:

25	March	1962
4	July	1776
7	May	1988

8.2 Write a function which accepts as input a list of numbers, and prints out the corresponding barchart using asterisks. For example, the input list (5 8 3 2) should give:

```
*****
********
***
**
```

Answers

8.1
```
( defun tabdates(list)
     ( cond
           ( (null list)    NIL )
           ( T (tabprint (head list))))
     )
)
( defun tabprint(date)
  (format T "~%~0,0T~A~10,0T~A~20,0T~A"
         (head date)(head(tail
  date))(head(tail(tail date))))
      (tabdates (tail list))
)
```

8.2
```
( defun barchart(list)
     ( cond
           ( (null list) NIL )
           ( T (onebar (head list)) )
     )
)
( defun onebar(x)
      (format T "~%~0,0,V,'*A" x "")
      (barchart (tail list) )
)
```

· 9 ·

Iterative Constructs

"Then you keep moving round, I suppose?" said Alice.
"Exactly so," said the Hatter: "as the things get used up."
"But what happens when you come to the beginning again?" Alice ventured to ask.

Alice's Adventures in Wonderland

So far I have deliberately shown Lisp as a language that handles all loops recursively. It's certainly true that *any* repetitive piece of code *can* be handled this way, but it doesn't follow that there isn't a better alternative. As a distinguished computer scientist, Christopher Strachey, once remarked, "Just because it is possible to push a pea up a mountain with your nose does not mean that is a sensible way of getting it there".

The problem with recursion is that it can be extremely expensive, both in terms of memory usage and time. If you look back to my **power** example it's quite easy to see why. First, the **power** function is repeatedly being called. On each call its current state must be saved, that is, a new return address plus the value it now returns. This will entail altering some stack pointers and transferring data to the memory cells referenced by them. That's time consuming and, as the stacks grow, space filling as well. Clearly the higher the power, the more serious these problems become, so that, in principle anyway, taking a high enough power could result in the machine crashing because it has run out of memory! Evidently, a conventional loop would be much more appropriate in this case. Common Lisp provides a number of looping functions, so that the programmer can make his own decisions about which mechanism is appropriate in a particular case.

loop

The simplest of these is **loop**. For instance:

```
( loop
             ( format T "~%Hello world" )
 )
```

will output the message "Hello world" indefinitely. Whatever functions form the body of **loop** are always evaluated *ad infinitum*. **loop** itself does not return a value (since it does not return!) and it appears to be a rather useless function because there seems to be no way out of it. However, appearances are deceptive . . .

return

A call to **return** will cause an exit from the current block (for the moment, I shall use the term 'block' as a synonym for 'function'; we shall see that it is more closely defined later). **return** takes an argument which is the value to be passed back.

So:

```
( loop
             ( format T "~%Hello world" )
             ( return T )
 )
```

would execute the loop only once and then return T. To be useful, of course, we need to **return** on some condition:

```
(setq count 10 )
( loop
             ( format T "~%Hello world" )
             ( setq count (dec count) )
             ( cond
                     ( (zerop count) (return T) )
                     ( T          T )
             )
 )
```

What happens is this: count is initialized to 0 and the loop is entered. The message is printed out and count is decremented by 1. Then a **cond** is entered, whose effect is to instigate a return (with the value T) when count is zero.

So you'd expect to get 10 "Hello world" messages followed by 'T'. And that's exactly what happens. But is it *really* what you'd expect? Well, if my explanation of the effect of **return** were precisely true the answer would be 'no', because it would return from the **cond** (the function which enclosed it), not from the **loop**. This wouldn't be much use, because it would have returned from **cond** anyway. The loop would continue to be recalculated indefinitely. So it's clear that **return** only returns from certain functions, which I have chosen to call 'blocks'. **loop** is just the first of these we have met.

do

The **do** function provides a neater way of handling the same kind of problem. Consider the following code:

```
( do
        (
                ( count 10 (dec count) )
        )
        ( (zerop count)    T  )
        ( format T "~%Hello world" )
)
```

If you run this you'll find it has exactly the same effect as the last **loop**. Following **do** there is first a list of three element lists. In this case, there is only one:

```
( count 10 (dec count) )
```

Its contents are a variable, a starting value for the variable and an action to take on the variable after every iteration. In this case the variable is 'count'. It starts at 10 and is decremented by 1 on every iteration. There may be any number of these lists, each describing how a different variable should change on every iteration.

This is followed by a list containing a test (here (zerop count)) and a result (T). If the test is true, the result is returned. Otherwise the *body* of the loop, that is, the remaining set of Lisp forms, is evaluated. Here, this is just (format T "~%Hello world"). Since the test is false for the first 10 iterations, the message is printed out 10 times.

The Size of a List

Let's examine a rather more useful problem. We'll write a function **size** which returns the number of atoms in a flat list which is passed to it. This is pretty easy. We need a variable called length, say, which holds the length of the list so far. This will start at zero. We also need a variable *part-x* whose initial value is *x* but which has its head removed on every iteration. When *part-x* is NIL, we've done:

```
( defun size(x)
        ( do
                (
                        ( length 0 (inc length) )
                        ( part-x x (tail part-x) )
                )
                ( (null part-x) length )
        )
)
```

An interesting feature of this **do** is that there is *no* body! All the necessary manipulation has been done in the variable initialization and incrementation section at the beginning. This is quite common, because many loops will only entail a series of consistent changes to variables. *Apparently*, these could be done either in the initialization section or in the body. For instance, I could rewrite **size**:

```
( defun size(x)
        ( do
                ( ( length 0 (inc length) )
                )
                ( (null part-x)     length )
                ( setq part-x    (tail part-x) )
        )
)
```

However, this would not be wise, because now I must (setq part-x x) before calling **size**. Otherwise Lisp will complain that it doesn't have a value for part-x when it first meets it in (null part-x). A moment's thought unearths another, very important, nugget of information. In the latter case, *part-x* would have global scope, having been referenced by **setq**; but in the first presentation of the function, *length* and *part-x* are arguments of **do** and are consequently bound in the **do**. You can easily confirm this by attempting to evaluate *length* or *part-x* after calling **size**. You'll get an 'unbound symbol' message, or something similar.

Thus we can see that by choosing and using our functions carefully we can overcome at least some of the software development problems to which I alluded in Chapter 5.

One last point; it's very easy to write the initialization line for *part-x* as:

```
( part-x x (tail x) )
```

I know, because that's exactly what I did when first testing this function. Then I wondered why my computer had apparently gone off in a sulk. Of course it had! It was repeatedly taking the tail of *x* which is *always* the same length. So *part-x* never became NIL. I am simply pointing out how careful you have to be about which variable is being referenced. I should have noticed this error straightaway by comparing it with the previous line:

```
( length   0   (inc length) )
```

Generally, the variable being initialized will also be the one to be manipulated, although Lisp is quite happy if this is not the case, as I discovered to my embarassment.

Iteration v. Recursion

It's interesting to compare this routine with a recursive equivalent:

```
( defun recursive-size(x)
        ( cond
                ( (null x) 0 )
                ( T (inc (recursive-size (tail x) ) ) ) )
        )
)
```

The definition is easy to analyse: if the list is null, then return zero. Otherwise return one more than the **size** of the tail.

This form of the function is clearly more compact. It is also much more intuitive. In the iterative case, we say, "do this, then do that and the answer will be produced". Here, we have little more than a hunch that the process *ought* to produce the correct answer because the definition is clearly correct. But we don't really want to think about the processes involved in the recursion. Nor should we; if we are convinced of the correctness of the definition, considering the actual process is a waste of time.

So it's often faster to write recursive code, but the *quid pro quo* is that we can expect it to execute more slowly and use more memory than the equivalent iterative code. This makes it particularly appropriate when we wish to develop an application fast, to demonstrate the look and feel of the software, prior to building a final agreed version. This is known as prototyping because of its similarity to the engineering habit of building working models before finally committing to a particular design. It's an area in which Lisp is particularly useful.

dotimes

do is clearly a very general function and there will be times when we do not need its full power. There are two more specific **do** style constructs. **dotimes** allows iteration over the integers from zero to some positive limit. For instance:

```
( dotimes
              ( count 10 T )
              ( format T "~%Hello world" )
)
```

will do the same job as all our other attempts to greet the world. Notice that the limit is *exclusive*. That is, the loop executes for count = 0, 1, 2 . . . 9 and exits as soon as count is 10 without evaluating the body.

dolist

dolist iterates over the elements of a list. It's easiest to see what's happening with an example:

```
( setq list '(a b c d) )
( dolist
              ( x list )
              ( format T "~%~A" x )
)
```

This generates:

```
A

B

C

D
```

In other words, each element of the list is bound to *x* in turn and the body of the loop is evaluated for every instance. We now have yet another way of writing **size**:

```
( defun size (x)
         ( dolist
               ( e    x )
               ( setq length  (inc length) )
         )
)
```

Each element of *x* is bound to *e* and *length* is incremented every time. Of course, this is not a nice solution because *length* is a global variable which must be bound to zero before each call to **size**. Also size does not return anything useful. In fact, it returns NIL. This is because there is an optional third argument in the list (e x) which I have not specified. This argument is returned by **dolist**. If it is omitted, NIL is returned, as here. So I could make **size** return length:

```
( defun size (x)
         ( dolist
          ( e    x    length )
          ( setq length (inc length) )
          )
)
```

but it's still an unpleasant implementation.

It's easy to think of more sensible uses for **dolist**. For example, suppose a list represents a sentence, each word being a Lisp atom. Let's imagine that we want to analyse the sentence for the number of different parts of speech (adjective, noun, verb and so on) that it contains. Further suppose we have written a set of predicates **nounp**, **adjectivep**, **verbp** etc. that return T if they are passed an appropriate word. **dolist** makes it easy to look at each word in turn:

```
( defun analyse (sentence)
         ( dolist
               ( word sentence )
               ( cond
                     ( (nounp word) (inc nouns) )
                     ( (adverbp word) (inc adverbs) )
                     ( (verbp word) (inc verbs) )
                         :
                       etc
                         :
                     ( T (format "~%~A is unknown" word) )
               )
         )
)
```

Again, nouns, verbs etc. are global variables that must be bound to zero before calling **analyse**. Wouldn't it be nice if we could form a list of the counts of the parts of speech and then make **analyse** return that ? Well, we can, but I'll defer discussing the mechanism temporarily.

Mapping

There are a number of functions that act in an iterative way on the elements of a list. Collectively, they are called the mapping functions. The difference between them lies in the way parts of the argument lists are selected and in what is returned.

mapcar

The simplest and most commonly used of these functions is **mapcar**. To see it in action try:

```
(setq x '(1  2  3  4) )
(mapcar  #'inc x)
```

You'll get:

```
(2  3  4  5)
```

Evidently, one has been added to each element of the list x. The arguments of **mapcar** are a function name (note that it is 'quoted' so that the interpreter does not attempt to evaluate it) and a list or set of lists (here just x). It operates by applying the function to the head of the list, then the head of the tail and so on, returning the list formed from the individual results.

  Now try:

```
(setq y '(10  11  12) )
(mapcar #'*  x y)
```

You get:

```
(10  22  36)
```

So Lisp has evaluated 1*10, 2*11 and 3*12 but has run out of partners for the 4 and has therefore done nothing with it. In other words, the iteration takes place over the length of the shortest list in the arguments.

  It's easy to see that this is a very useful function if you are designing a spreadsheet—multiplying two columns together becomes trivial if those columns are represented as lists, for instance—but it's also very convenient for any kind of matrix manipulation, or for dealing with bit patterns held as lists. Suppose, for example that we want to flip the bits of a binary number held as, say:

```
(1 1 0 0 0 1 1 1)
```

For one bit this is easy:

```
( defun flip (bit)
     ( cond
          ( (= bit 1) 0 )
          ( T    1 )
     )
)
```

So, for the list we have:

```
(defun ones-complement (word)
        (mapcar #'flip word)
)
```

and now we can write:

```
(ones-complement '(1 1 0 0 0 1 1 1) )
```

The remaining mapping functions come in two categories: obscure and danger-ous. Some manipulate the lists and their successive tails, which is obscure because it's very difficult to think of practical cases where this might be useful. Others manipulate their arguments in place, which is dangerous because the returned value is not distinct from the argument. Consequently, great clarity of thought about exactly what is being altered is required. These are dangerous waters for the beginner and many professional programmers frown upon the use of such mechanisms precisely because they break down the essential func-tionality of Lisp. I shall therefore forgo further comment on them.

Exercises 9

9.1 Rewrite your answer to Exercise 7.1 iteratively.
9.2 Write a function **newlines**(n) to print out n new lines.
9.3 Rewrite your answer to Exercise 8.1 iteratively.
9.4 Rewrite your answer to Exercise 8.2 iteratively.
9.5 Write a function **trans**(*list*) which transforms a list of months, held as numbers, into corresponding lists of words, e.g. (1 2 3) becomes (January February March).

Answers

9.1 My answer uses **tsil** from Exercise 5.

```
( setq x NIL )
( defun getlist()
      ( loop
             ( setq x (cons (read) x))
             ( cond
                    ( (= (head x) 0) (return) )
                    ( T T )
             )
      )
      ( setq x (tsil(tail x)))
)
```

9.2
```
( defun newlines(n)
      ( dotimes
             ( count n T )
             ( terpri )
      )
)
```

```
9.3      ( defun tabdates(list)
             ( dolist
               ( date list )
               ( format T "~%~0,0T~A~10,0T~A~20,0T~A"
                 (head date)(head(tail date))
                            (head(tail(tail date))))
             )
         )

9.4      ( defun barchart(list)
             ( dolist
                 ( bar list )
                 ( format T "~%~0,0,V,'*A" bar "")
             )
         )

9.5      ( defun no-month (no)
             ( cond
                 ( (= no  1) 'january)
                 ( (= no  2) 'february)
                    :
                    :
                 ( (= no 12) 'december))
             )
         )
         ( defun trans (list)
                 ( mapcar #' no-month list)
         )
```

· 10 ·

More About Program Control

"I only said 'if'!" poor Alice pleaded in a piteous tone.

Through the Looking-Glass

Lisp has a rich set of mechanisms for handling program control, very few of which we have met so far. We'll remedy this oversight now, looking first at some more conditional functions. To date we've only seen one, **cond**. There is no absolute need for any others, but there are times when code can be made clearer using other, less general, functions. Common Lisp provides the following.

if

if takes three arguments. The first is a predicate. If this returns T, the second is evaluated and returned. Otherwise the third is evaluated and returned. So:

```
( if condition x y )
```

is equivalent to:

```
IF condition THEN x ELSE y
```

in a more verbose language.

The third argument is optional, so:

```
( if condition x )
```

can be read as:

```
IF condition THEN x
```

In that case, NIL is returned if the condition is false.

We now have a simpler way of writing the loop example in Chapter 8:

```
( setq count 10 )
( loop
      ( format T "~%Hello world" )
      ( setq count (dec count) )
      ( if (zerop count) (return T) )
)
```

when

when is like **if** in that it performs a test. It differs in that **if** would evaluate a single function on the basis of the test, whereas **when** evaluates a block of functions (like a **loop** body). Thus, in the above example, **if** could be replaced by **when**.

The general form of a **when** is:

```
( when condition body )
```

and 'body', which is any set of Lisp forms, is evaluated only if 'condition' is T.

unless

This is simply the inverse form of **when**. It has the form:

```
( unless condition body )
```

and 'body' is evaluated unless 'condition' is T.

These two forms are not often strictly necessary, because of the possibility of putting the block to be executed somewhere else (as in the initialization section of a **do**). However, **unless** is useful as an inverse of **if**.

case

Most modern languages have a form whose effect is to select one from a group of possible actions according to the value of a particular variable. It's often called a 'case' or 'switch' statement. Common Lisp has a **case** function that models this feature. However, it is somewhat more powerful than most of its contemporaries as we shall see shortly. For the moment, though, we'll examine a rather simple, if common, example to get a feel for the function's structure.

Suppose that you're designing a database management system. The user will be given a menu of options on entering the system. These will include such operations as 'create a file', 'find a record', 'delete a record', 'delete a file' and so on. A conventional (and primitive) approach is to number the menu options and ask the user to enter the number corresponding to his selection. You can then write a Lisp function called **select** that will call another function to carry out the task:

```
( defun select (option)
     ( case option
            ( 1 ( create ) )
            ( 2 ( find ) )
            ( 3 ( del ) )
                    :
                    :
         )
    )
```

The arguments of **case** are a *key* (in this instance, option) and a set of lists. Each list contains a possible value for the key and an action (typically a function call) that is to be taken should the key and the value match. If no match occurs, **case** *returns NIL*.

  You can check this out by writing trivial versions of **create**, **find**, and **del** that merely print messages.

  You might expect it to be possible to replace the 1, 2 and 3 by strings "create", "find" and "delete". This won't work, though. The problem is our old friend **eq**. Strings are not stored uniquely, so a match may not be found. (Actually, **case** uses another comparator function **eql**, but the same analysis applies.) Atoms are OK of course:

```
( defun select (option)
     ( case option
            ( 'create (create) )
            ( 'find    (find) )
            ( 'delete (del) )
         )
    )
```

The user need not be aware of the problem, because **read** will return an atom DELETE to **select** in a form such as:

```
( select (read) )delete
```

Synonyms

Now for the clever bit. The key specifications (so far just constants 1, 2, 3 or atoms 'create, 'find and 'delete) may be lists. If so, **case** searches for a match within the list.

  That means we could write:

```
( defun select (option)
     ( case option
            ( (create make start)  (create) )
            ( (find search locate)  (find) )
            ( (delete remove)  (del) )
         )
    )
```

Now the system will respond to a range of similar keywords. For instance, the user need not remember that the keyword to select a particular record is 'find'. He can use 'search' or 'locate' instead. This makes it relatively easy to build a user interface that, while not providing a true natural English interaction, is at least fairly forgiving.

Defaults

While it is possible to deal with invalid entries using the fact that **case** returns NIL if no match is found, it would be more convenient to handle defaults from inside the function. The constant T can be used as a key specification to do this in much the same way as it is in a **cond**. It is given the synonym OTHERWISE for readability. If these defaults are used, they must appear as the final list in the **case**. So we might write:

```
( defun select (option)
    ( case option
            ( (create make start)  (create) )
            ( (find search locate) (find) )
            ( (delete remove)  (del) )
            ( OTHERWISE
                    (format T "I don't know the word ~a"
                                        option) )
    )
)
```

Some New Control Constructs

if, **when**, **unless** and **case** provide us with no completely new tools. Their features could be mimicked by appropriate calls to **cond**. In this sense, they do no more than sprinkle a little syntactic sugar over our code, making it easier to read, and, by the same token, to write. The next few functions, however, genuinely add strings to our bow (if I may be allowed to mix my metaphors outrageously).

let

First, we'll examine the **let** function. Anyone familiar with BASIC will guess that **let** performs assignments; you should by now have enough of a feel for the Lisp philosophy to know that it will do more besides. Here's an exploratory example of its use:

```
(defun testlet()
    ( setq x 2 )
    ( setq y 3 )
    ( let
            (
                    ( x 5 )
                    ( y 10 )
            )
            ( format T "~%x is ~a y is ~a" x y )
    )
    ( format T "~%x is ~a y is ~a" x y )
)
```

The arguments of **let** consist of a list consisting of a list of pairs, each of which performs an assignment (thus x is bound to 5, y to 10) and a body. The body is any set of Lisp forms. These are evaluated in turn and the value of the last of them is returned. In this instance, there is only one form in the body:

```
( format T "~%x is ~a y is ~a" x y )
```

which returns NIL to testlet, which in turn returns it to the caller.

If you invoke testlet from the interpreter top level you will get the display:

```
(testlet)
x is 5 y is 10
x is 2 y is 3
NIL
```

It's immediately apparent that the x and y assigned in the **let** are not the same as those referred to by **setq**. In other words, **let** allows us to make local assignments. This overcomes some of the problems that I raised in Chapter 5. Now if only we could localize function definitions . . .

flet

Well, we can. The function **flet** does for functions what **let** does for variables. Again, we'll examine an exploratory example in a moment, but first I must make a confession. Very early in this book, I invented two functions called **inc** and **dec** and have used them freely ever since. In fact, I need not have done so, because they are Lisp primitives, although they are called **1+** and **1−** respectively. However, I could not have written:

```
( defun 1+(x)
      ( + x 1 )
)
```

without incurring the displeasure of the interpreter. *Exactly* what happens if you try this is implementation dependent. My interpreter warns me that I am trying to redefine a Lisp primitive and gives me the option of doing so. I would have to be very sure of my ground (or very foolhardy) to carry on. But **flet** allows me to make *local* function redefinitions which are, of course, much more controllable. This will act as a suitable illustration:

```
( defun testflet()
      ( flet
            (
                  (
                        1+ (x)
                              ( + x 10 )
                  )
                  (
                        1- (x)
                              ( - x 10 )
                  )
            )
            ( format T "~% ~a" (1+ 100) )
            ( format T "~% ~a" (1- 100) )
      )
)
```

The first argument of **flet** is a list, each element of which is a function definition. This is followed by a body of forms to be evaluated in turn, the value of the final form being returned, as for **let**. If you evaluate the above, you'll get:

```
110
90
```

since **1+** and **1−** have been redefined to alter their arguments by 10 instead of 1. Subsequently writing:

```
( 1+ 7)
```

will yield:

```
8
```

indicating that the primitives have not been tampered with, as predicted.

What happens, though, if the function being redefined appears in the new definition? For example, if I wish to redefine + so that $(+ \; x \; y)$ will evaluate to $2x+y$, is the following valid?

```
( flet
     (
              ( + ( x y )
                   ( + x x y )
              )
     )
     :
     :
)
```

The answer is 'yes'. That might strike you as odd, since it means that **flet** must distinguish between the '+' of the new definition and the '+' that is the existing primitive. It does so because the new function name does not mean anything to the interpreter until the function definition has been completed. In fact, all the local functions are effectively defined in parallel, not in sequence.

There is another function, **labels**, whose syntax is identical to that of **flet** and whose action differs only in that the redefinition applies recursively. If you replace **flet** above with **labels** the result would be an error message pointing out that there are too many arguments to +. Of course there are; I've redefined it to have two arguments and then used it with three!

prog1 to progn

Thus far, I have been rather imprecise about saying how Lisp handles *sequences* of function calls or other forms. You might expect it to evaluate each form in turn and return the value of the last in the sequence, which is what happens in a **let** or **flet**.

The functions **prog1**, **prog2** and **progn** can be used to make just such evaluation rules explicit. The suffix 1, 2 or n indicates which function evaluation is returned—the first, second or nth (i.e. last).

Try:

```
( defun testprog ( x y )
     ( progn
          ( format T "~%x is ~a" x )
          ( format T "~%y is ~a" y )
          ( * x y )
     )
)
```

As you can see, the arguments of a **progn** are just an indefinite sequence of Lisp forms. Try:

```
( testprog 3 4 )
```

You'll get:

```
x is 3
y is 4
12
```

No surprise here; each form is evaluated and the last value returned. Now replace **progn** with **prog1** and repeat the test:

```
x is 3
y is 4
NIL
```

Each form is still evaluated, but this time the value of the first function (NIL because **format** returns NIL) is returned.

Similarly, **prog2** will return the value of the second function.

The Lambda Notation

Try this:

```
(
          ( lambda (x)
               ( + x 5 )
          )
          10
)
```

You'll get:

```
15
```

At one level, it's clear what's happened. 10 has been added to 5. Big deal. However, there's clearly more to it than that.

A lambda expression consists of lambda, a lambda list and a body. Here the lambda list is (x) which looks suspiciously like a parameter list in a function definition. That's because it *is* one. The body is the function description. Forming a list from a lambda expression and a set of actual parameters causes these to be bound to the formal parameters (here 10 is bound to *x*) and the function to be evaluated. In fact, this is Lisp's internal mechanism for handling functions. **defun** forms equivalent lambda expressions to which values are bound at execution time.

From the user's point of view, lambda allows the creation of anonymous functions. If I hadn't just described **flet**, it might be tempting to use it for this purpose, since it is another way around the redefinition problem. However, I have a personal distaste for nameless functions because they present unnecessary hurdles to the reader of a piece of code; the clue that should be provided by the function name is missing.

In a delightful, if food-fixated, book entitled *"The Little Lisper"*, Daniel P. Friedman writes: "[The lambda notation] is as useful as a screen door on a submarine sandwich." I'm with him.

So why have I mentioned it at all? Partly because you'll see it in other people's code, but, more importantly, if you get Lisp to display a previously stored function it will actually print the equivalent lambda expression. The mechanism for generating such a listing for a function called **func** is:

```
( print #'func )
```

The symbol pair #' is analogous to the single quote mark to force self-evaluation of a symbol in a form like:

```
( setq x 'a )
```

You might also expect the form:

```
#'func
```

to be evaluated by **eval** to generate the appropriate display, as indeed it will.

Exercises 10

10.1 Rewrite your answer to Exercise 4.2 using **if**.
10.2 Rewrite your answer to Exercise 7.1 using **unless**.
10.3 Rewrite your answer to Exercise 8.2 using **unless**.
10.4 Rewrite your answer to Exercise 8.5 using **case**.

Answers

```
10.1    ( defun fact(n)
            ( if   ( zerop n )
                     1      (* n (fact (- n 1))))
            )
        )

10.2    ( setq x NIL )
        ( defun getlist()
            ( setq temp (read) )
            ( unless
                (zerop temp)
                ( setq x (cons temp x) )
                (getlist)
            )
        )
```

10.3   (defun barchart(list)
              (unless
                   (null list)

                   (format T "~%~0,0,V,'*A" (head list) "")
                   (barchart (tail list))

)
)

10.4   (defun no-month (no)
              (case no
                   (1 'january)
                   (2 'february)
                      :
                      :
                   (12 'december)
)
)
        (defun trans (list)
              (mapcar #'no-month list)
)

· 11 ·

File Handling

"I only meant that I didn't understand," said Alice. "Why one to come and one to go?"

"Don't I tell you?" the King repeated impatiently. "I must have two—to fetch and carry. One to fetch, and one to carry."

Through the Looking-Glass

The computer language designer or implementor (or both) is always presented with a serious problem when he considers how to deal with disk files. It is that the language does not interface directly with the disk (or other mass storage device) at all, but rather with the operating system, whose responsibility it is to get stuff written in a retrievable way. So the problem becomes "How can we talk to any number of idiosyncratic operating systems, whose logical file structures and organization may be quite different, in a completely consistent way?"

Some language designers, notably those of Algol 60, solved this problem very economically by ignoring it altogether and simply not offering any kind of I/O interface. This allowed total consistency within the language definition, but implementors free rein. Consequently every Algol 60 implementation looked different at the I/O level and inevitably, code was not portable between them.

The designers of Common Lisp have made a remarkable effort to provide genuine portability across a wide range of systems; and they have succeeded, at the expense of some rather obscure structures that the programmer must be aware of to use the system properly. In other words they have sacrificed simplicity for portability.

However, as long as we keep our heads, there is really nothing in what follows to cause us undue turmoil.

Pathnames

Common Lisp uses a mechanism called the *pathname* to describe a particular file system interface. To see this at work type:

```
*default-pathname-defaults*
```

A system variable of the above name is evaluated. On my system the result is:

```
#S(PATHNAME HOST :MSDOS DEVICE "E" DIRECTORY NIL NAME
    NIL TYPE NIL VERSION NIL )
```

It's clear that this tells us something about the nature of the file system: that the host operating system is MSDOS, that the logged on disk drive is E and that there are no directory, filename, filetype or version parameters in force. Bear in mind that, as the variable name suggests, these are the *default* values of the *default* pathname. By implication, there can be other values and other pathnames. For the moment, we shall restrict ourselves to examining how to change the values in this pathname only.

merge-pathnames

Now try this:

```
(merge-pathnames "demo.txt")
```

This is returned:

```
#S(PATHNAME HOST :MSDOS DEVICE "E" DIRECTORY NIL NAME
    "DEMO" TYPE "TXT" VERSION "NEWEST")
```

'DEMO' and 'TXT' have been merged into the default pathname and the version has become 'NEWEST'. *Now* we have a complete file description; so how do we make use of it?

Streams

In common with most other modern languages, Common Lisp uses the operating system concept of a *stream* to identify the source or destination of a file transfer. In some I/O functions the stream is obligatory and in others defaults are used if it is missing. For example:

```
(read)
```

clearly specifies no stream and we know it works, taking its input from the console. On the other hand:

```
(format T "Hello world~%")
```

does (in a roundabout way) tell the system which stream to use. The 'T' identifies the stream associated with a system variable *terminal-io*. With **format**, a stream is necessary. With **read**, it's an option. That is why all calls to **format** used thus far have had the (up to now) unexplained 'T'. **merge-pathnames** returns a pathname which is linked in an implementation independent way to a stream. The #S preceding the list indicates that a pathname is a structure (see Chapter 13).

Opening and Closing Files

Most languages require three distinct phases to a file handling operation. First, the file must be opened. Second, data are transferred to (or from) it. Finally, the file is closed. You can perform these operations conventionally in Lisp, but there's a nicer way to operate. The function **with-open-file** will open a file, perform file transfers and close it again without the programmer having to do so explicitly. Here's a rather primitive example:

```
(defun file ()
    (with-open-file ( out (merge-pathnames "demo.txt")
                          :direction :output
                          :if-does-not-exist :create
                          :if-exists :append
                    )
        (format out "Test line 1~%")
        (format out "Test line 2~%")
        (format out "Test line 3~%")
    )
)
```

The first argument to the function is a list containing a stream evaluation and some other stuff that I'll come to shortly. The stream evaluation is a kind of implicit **setq**. In the example, 'out' is given the value returned by **merge-pathname**, which, we already know, gives the required file description.

There follow a set of arguments which evidently define the file type and specify the behaviour of the program in all eventualities. Translated, it says:

"The file is open for output. If no file of this name exists, create one. Otherwise, append the new data to the existing file."

Keyword Arguments

We have met a function argument preceded by a colon once before (where?) but it was not really worth investigating then. Here, though, such arguments assume an importance that means I can no longer prevaricate.

An argument preceded by a colon is called a *keyword argument*. Its significance is that (normally) it consists of two parts, a descriptor and a description.

Since the first defines what the second refers to, the order of keyword arguments is immaterial. For example, I might write a function called **plot** to plot a point in a Cartesian graph space. I can either say "The first argument is x and the second is y" so that a call of the form (plot 12 20) will plot a point at (12,20) or I could write the function using keyword arguments and call it with:

```
(plot :x 12
      :y 20)
```

or:

```
(plot :y 20
      :x 12)
```

The clear advantage of the latter structure is that the user need not remember an arbitrary order of function arguments. I shall discuss how to *write* functions with keyword arguments later.

The Body

The second argument to **with-open-file** is the body. This example bears little comment. Clearly, it outputs three lines of text to the stream called 'out' which is in turn linked to the file 'demo.txt'. The important point here is that *however* the body is left, **with-open-file** closes the file for you.

Other Keyword Arguments

There are a number of keyword arguments and values that I have not yet shown. For example the pair:

```
:if-exists      :error
```

can be used to issue an error message (perhaps 'File already exists') if you don't want to modify an existing file. Also, a file may be made bidirectional with:

```
:direction :io
```

Numerous other possibilities exist and there is little point in listing them all since they appear in your implementation manual. I shall content myself with remarking that if the file is to be read, no keyword arguments need be specified at all, because the defaults are:

```
:direction      :input
:if-does-not-exist    :error
:element-type      :string-char
```

I mention the keyword :element-type for completeness, but it's unlikely that you'd want to change it from :string-char, which just indicates that the currency of data transfer is the character.

Getting the File Back

Now try this:

```
(defun infile ( )
       (with-open-file (in (merge-pathnames "demo.txt"))
             (setq x (read-line in))
             (setq y (read-line in))
             (setq z (read-line in))
             (format "~a ~a ~a" x y z)
       )
)
```

Nothing remarkable here. Note, though, the use of **read-line** rather than **read**. What will happen if you use **read** ? (and why?).

Of course, another call to **read-line**, say with:

```
(setq w (read-line in) )
```

will result in an error message such as "Attempt to read past end of file".

There are several ways around this problem. Perhaps the simplest is to have the file length as the first entry, thus:

```
3
Test line 1
test line 2
test line 3
```

Now we can use **dotimes** to read the file:

```
(defun infile ( )
     (with-open-file (in (merge-pathnames "demo.txt") )
          (dotimes (record-no (read in) )
              (format T "~%~a ~a" record-no (read-line in) )
          )
     )
)
```

This will give:

```
0 Test line 1
1 Test line 2
2 Test line 3
NIL
```

(Remember that **dotimes** iterates from 0 to one less than the count. The NIL is returned by **with-open-file**.)

EOF-ERROR-P and EOF-VALUE

It may not be convenient to keep a record of the length of a file. The obvious alternative is to use the end of file marker that must delimit the file. Of course, the precise nature of the delimiter is system dependent. As usual, Common Lisp has a way around this little difficulty.

There are two further optional arguments to **read** (and **read-line**). These are EOF-ERROR-P and EOF-VALUE. The default value of EOF-ERROR-P (which, as you'd expect, is a predicate) is T and this indicates to the system that it is to print an error message on encountering the end of a file. If it is NIL, however, no error is signalled, but **read** returns whatever is the value of EOF-VALUE.

Thus a construction like:

```
(read in NIL NIL)
```

means:

"Read an object from the stream *in*. Do not signal end of file overtly, but return NIL instead."

We could use **loop** to read and print the entire file like this:

```
(defun infile( )
    (with-open-file (in (merge-pathnames "demo.txt") )
        (loop
                (setq x (read-line in NIL NIL) )
                (if x
                        (format T '"~%~a" x)
                        (return)
                )
            )
        )
)
```

since *x* will be treated as T if it is non-NIL.

Exercises 11

11.1 A list, called storefile, itself consists of a set of lists. Write a function **purge**(*entry*) to create a new list called purgedfile which deletes from the old one those elements containing the element *entry*. For example, if (purge 2) is applied to the storefile

```
(3  5  7)
(1  2  3)
(6  8  9)
```

then it generates the purgedfile

```
(3  5  7)
(6  8  9)
```

Include **purge** in a program to read a file called oldfile into the global variable storefile, perform the purge and write the result back to newfile. (*Hint*: you may need the function **element-p** from Exercise 4.1. You will also have to write **getfile** and **putfile** to handle the file transfers.)

Answers

11.1   (setq storefile NIL)
         (setq purgedfile NIL)
         (getfile "oldfile")
         (purge 2)
         (putfile "newfile")
         (defun getfile(name)
             (with-open-file (in (merge-pathnames name))
                 (loop
                         (setq temp (read in NIL NIL))
                         (if temp
                             (setq storefile (append
                                     storefile (list temp)))
                             (return)
)
)
)
)
         (defun purge(entry)
             (dolist
                 (record storefile)
                 (unless
                     (element-p entry record)
                     (setq purgedfile (append
                             purgedfile (list record)))
)
)
)
         (defun putfile(name)
             (with-open-file(out (merge-pathnames name)
                             :direction :output
                             :if-does-not-exist :create
)
                 (dolist
                     (record purgedfile)
                     (format out "~A~%" record)
)
)
)

(Chapter 12 provides a way of doing all this without creating the temporary lists,
by alternately reading from the old file and writing to the new one.)

· 12 ·
Data Structures

So she went on, wondering more and more at every step, as everything turned into a tree the moment she came up to it.

Through the Looking-Glass

Lisp's primary data structure, the list, is, as we've already seen, a pretty useful construction. It's possible to argue that there is no need for any other. However, this is much like saying that we don't need iterative functions or that we could do without **let**. Of course we *could*, but life would be made more difficult for us.

In this chapter we'll examine some ways in which lists can model other structures and some completely new data handling techniques.

Association Lists

An association list is a list of pairs of entries. The first of a pair is called the *key* and the second is the *datum*. An example of its use might be in holding passport records, whose form might be:

Name
Nationality
Birth date
Eye colour
Hair colour
Height
Sex

In a conventional database language (like dBASEIII), the order of these entries (and, indeed, their size and number) would be specified when the file is created and cannot be easily altered from then on. As we shall see, Common Lisp allows almost unlimited flexibility in this context. Each of the attributes specified above (Name, Nationality and so on) will be a key and the corresponding details will form the data.

pairlis

One way to create such a set of relationships is to use the function **pairlis** like this:

```
(setq passport (pairlis '(name nationality birth-date
eye-colour hair-colour height sex)
                        '(smith british sept-9-45 brown
black 174 male)
                )
)
```

This returns:

```
( (SEX . MALE) (HEIGHT . 174) (HAIR-COLOUR . BLACK)
  (EYE-COLOUR . BROWN) (BIRTH-DATE . SEPT-9-45)
  (NATIONALITY . BRITISH) (NAME . SMITH) )
```

There are two points to notice about this result. First, **pairlis** does not guarantee to form the pairs in the order they were entered. Of course, this doesn't matter since a key and its data appear together. Second, the pairs have been created in a new way—using the *dot notation*.

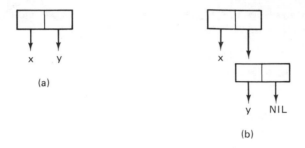

FIGURE 9. How $(x . y)$ differs from $(x y)$: (a) $(x . y)$; (b) $(x y)$.

The Dot Notation

The list $(x . y)$ is not the same as the list $(x y)$. The difference lies in the way the lists are constructed. If you write:

```
(cons 'x '(y) )
```

x is consed on to the existing list (y) and the result is as shown in Figure 9 (b). However if you **cons** two atoms:

```
(cons 'x 'y)
```

the result is figure 9 (a). The dot notation merely provides a mechanism for distinguishing between these two structures.

assoc

The function **assoc** can now be used to extract information from the structure. Its arguments are a key and an association list. It returns the first dotted pair it finds with the stated key. Thus:

```
(assoc 'hair-colour passport)
```

returns:

```
(HAIR-COLOUR . BLACK)
```

If no matching key is found, **assoc** returns NIL.

rassoc

Given a datum, rather than a key, **rassoc** will return the appropriate dotted pair. For instance:

```
(rassoc 'brown passport)
```

returns:

```
(EYE-COLOUR . BROWN)
```

Again, it is the first such pair that **rassoc** latches on to. If we had changed the hair colour from black to brown, **rassoc** would have returned:

```
(HAIR-COLOUR . BROWN)
```

Since the order of the data returned by **pairlis** is undefined this is the answer to the question, "What is an entry whose attribute is 'brown'?"; **rassoc** provides no information about any ambiguities caused by multiple entries with the same value. Indeed, neither does **assoc**, although you might expect the keys to be unique. Even this isn't always true though . . .

acons

We can add new information to an association list using **acons**, which returns the old list with a new head. Let's add our passport holder's profession:

```
(setq passport (acons 'profession 'accountant passport) )
```

Now, the flexibility of this organization begins to appear. Clearly, we can add indefinitely many attributes to the passport list whenever we like. What's more, there is no need for a change to affect anybody else's passport record, as would have to be the case if all such records had a predefined format. While passport information is restricted to the bare necessities and it isn't likely that we would want to add fields in this way, a moment's thought suggests numerous examples where this facility is very useful. For example, a personnel record grows with the length of time an employee remains with a company; he adds to his qualifications, takes on new responsibilities, his health record is modified, and so on.

We can also use **acons** to alter the current state of an entry in a record. Suppose our passport holder were to change his nationality by becoming a naturalized Australian:

```
(setq passport (acons 'nationality 'australian
    passport) )
```

will make the necessary modification. Of course, there are now two nationality entries, but the first will describe our friend as Australian and that's the one **assoc** will pick up. It is possible, but not especially good practice, to alter, rather than add to, an association list with:

setf

Like **setq**, this is an assignment procedure. However, it is much more general. To see why, think about the general process of assignment. It has two stages:

1. Find the object under consideration.
2. Update it.

setf provides a completely universal mechanism for dealing with stage 1, so it can be used in any assignment operation (thus, incidentally, making **setq** redundant). Its general form is:

```
(setf place value)
```

In our example the 'place' is the tail of (NATIONALITY.BRITISH), which, in turn, is (assoc 'nationality passport) so we need to write:

```
(setf (tail (assoc 'nationality passport)) 'australian)
```

AUSTRALIAN is returned but, of course, this is not so important as the side effect that **setf** has of modifying *passport*.

There are two reasons why this is not the preferred *modus operandi*. First, as I have pointed out elsewhere, functions that are invoked for their side effects are frowned upon because using them destroys the functional nature of Lisp and can make debugging more difficult. Second, on a more pragmatic note, the method destroys the information that this gentleman *used* to be British. A piece of his history has disappeared. Since he is an accountant, he might phrase it a little differently. He would say that an audit trail has been lost. In any event, that information was potentially useful. Our only valid reason for removing it can be that memory is limited.

Database Manipulation

Clearly, the foregoing hints at the possibility of building a powerful and flexible database with remarkably little programming effort. Let's look at a particular function that a database manager should include to illustrate the point. We'll call it **modify-record**. It will take two dotted pairs as arguments and search through a file of association lists looking for a match with the first. If it finds one, it will **acons** the second on to the target association list. Thus, if we start with the file:

```
( (surname . allen)(forename . john)(tel-no . 76392) )
( (surname . pritchard)(forename . jeremy)(tel-no .
42638) )
( (surname . smith)(forename . mary)(tel-no . 15836) )
```

and write:

```
( modify-record (forename . jeremy) (tel-no . 58431) )
```

the file should become:

```
( (surname . allen)(forename . john)(tel-no . 76392) )
( (tel-no . 58431)(surname . pritchard)(forename .
jeremy)
   (tel-no . 42638) )
( (surname . smith)(forename . mary)(tel-no . 15836) )
```

In fact, things will be easier if we have two files. Data will be read from the first and written without alteration to the second except for the case (if it exists) where the match is found. Here the revised association list is written out. We'll call the files 'data.old' and 'data.new'. Unfortunately a single **with-open-file** can open only one file so we'll have to nest a pair of them :

```
(defun modify-record(target revision)
       (with-open-file    (in (merge-pathnames
                              "data.old") )
         (with-open-file (out (merge-pathnames
                              "data.new")
```

```
                              :direction :output
                              :if-exists :error
          )
       (loop
            (setq record (read in NIL NIL) )
            (if record
                  (format out "~A~%"
                         (new-record target
                                    revision) )
                  (return)
            )
         )
       )
     )
)
```

This bears a remarkable similarity to the **infile** function in Chapter 11. To keep things simple, I've introduced a function **new-record** which will return either the original record or the modified one depending on whether this is the 'target' record.

```
(defun new-record (target revision)
      (if (equal target (assoc (head target)
                                       record)
            (acons (head revision)(tail revision)
                                       record)
            record
       )
)
```

There are several points to notice here. First, we don't need to pass *record* as an argument to **new-record** because it is global. (Why?) Second, **assoc** takes the first atom of a dotted pair as its first argument (hence (head target)) and returns the complete dotted pair. This is then compared with target using **equal**. This primitive differs from **eq** in that it compares *lists* for equality. More precisely, it returns T if its arguments are structurally identical. Third, **acons** requires the elements of the dotted pair to be added as separate arguments. This means I had to write (head revision) and (tail revision) so that it would have been easier to provide these elements as separate arguments. The reason I didn't do this was that the arguments to **modify-record** would then have been unnecessarily inconsistent.

Trees

So far, we have considered only structures that are implemented directly in Lisp, but it's quite easy to model extrinsic data organizations. A good example of this is the *tree*, which is much beloved of computer scientists because it can be used in a wide range of applications. A tree is a data structure consisting of *nodes* and *branches*. Each node (except the *root*) has exactly one entry branch and may have zero or more exit branches. Figure 10 shows an example.

Why should this structure be so attractive? There are two general reasons. The first is that it *partitions* data. A disk directory is usually tree structured, for

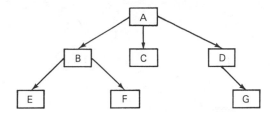

FIGURE 10. A tree with root 'A' and leaves 'E', 'F', 'C' and 'G'.

instance. We'll see a more interesting example of the power of partitioning shortly. The second reason is that the tree lends itself to recursive programming techniques very easily. This is because every part of the tree is itself a tree. For example, in Figure 10, if we remove all but the left branch from 'A' we are left with a tree whose root is 'B'.

Binary Trees

If no more than two branches exit from any node in a tree, it is said to be *binary*. Clearly such a restriction makes analysis easier, but it turns out that any tree, however complex, can be modelled on a binary tree, so there's really no need to worry about the general case. A proof of this result would be inappropriate here; if you're interested, see *The Art of Computer Programming*, Volume 3—*Sorting and Searching*, by Donald E. Knuth. In any event, we'll concern ourselves only with binary trees.

The Searching Problem

To see them at work, let's look at some solutions to a problem we have so far taken for granted—that of searching a data structure efficiently. We've already seen that our association list is searched left to right for the target data. If this were not so, some of the algorithms I have suggested for manipulating databases would not work. That can work against us if the list is sufficiently long and the target data are towards the end. Suppose that the passport data were arranged in a tree whose structure is shown in Figure 11. This looks slightly odd until you realize that a simple rule is being used to determine where to place an attribute: if it is alphabetically before a node, move left through the tree. If it is after the node, move right. This produces a symmetrical structure only if nodes are entered in the right order. For instance, If I had started with 'Birth date' at the root, there would be no left subtree at all. Given this proviso, however, we can see that a tree search can be made very fast. Suppose we are looking for 'Hair'. This lies before 'Height' and so must be in the left subtree; but it is after 'Eyes' and so must be to the right of that. At each comparison, half the remaining tree is lopped off and need be considered no further. Incidentally, a symmetrical binary tree is said to be *balanced*.

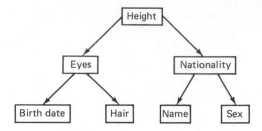

FIGURE 11. The passport details as a tree.

Implementing a Binary Tree

Having thought, at least in principle, about the benefits of this organization, let's try to implement it. We can think about a node as having three characteristics—a value, a left subtree and a right subtree. Clearly we can write this as a list:

```
(value left-subtree right-subtree)
```

Wait a bit though—if the node is the root, this is a description of the *whole* tree and, even if it's not, it's a description of *some* tree (it's a recursive structure, remember?). So this list describes a tree rather than just a node. We need only to define *value* as meaning 'the value of the tree' rather than just 'the value of the node'. In fact this is a common idea—the value of the root node is said to be the value of the tree.

We can now begin to make some function definitions for manipulating trees:

```
(defun value (x)
        (head x)
)
```

That's trivial; we're simply saying that if *x* is a tree, the head of *x* is its value. Similarly:

```
(defun left-subtree (x)
        ( head (tail x) )
)
```

and:

```
(defun right-subtree (x)
            (head (tail (tail x)))
)
```

Growing a Tree

Now let's look at how to add a node to an existing tree. We'll assume that the data to be entered are numeric, for no better reason than that we can then use the comparison predicates =, > and <. In more interesting cases we might first have to describe appropriate comparator functions, but otherwise the mechanisms will be the same.

First, we'll describe the function **make-tree** which forms a tree from a value and two sub-trees:

```
(defun make-tree (value left right)
        (list value left right)
    )
```

This is just the synthetic equivalent of the analytic functions **value, left-subtree** and **right-subtree**.

Now we need to consider the range of possibilites for the current state of the tree and the node, *x* that we want to add.

The tree could be empty:

```
( (null tree) (make-tree x NIL NIL) )
```

In this case, we simply install the node and set both subtrees to NIL.

The root node could be the same as the value we're trying to add:

```
( (= x (value tree) ) tree)
```

This time we simply return the tree, since we can't allow duplicate entries.

x may be less than the values of the tree:

```
( ( < x (value tree) ) (grow-tree x (left-subtree tree) ) )
```

Actually, this is an over-simplication; we must make a new tree, otherwise only the immediate change is returned (i.e. every call to **grow-tree** would return a list of the form (x NIL NIL)—not very useful). It's easy to see how we can use **make-tree** for this. We simply pass it the value of the tree, the new left subtree and the original right subtree, which is unaltered:

```
( (< x (value tree) ) (make-tree
                              (value-tree)
                              (grow-tree x (left-subtree
                                        tree) )
                              (right-subtree tree)
                      )
)
```

The only remaining condition (i.e. T) is that *x* is greater than the value of the tree and in that case we grow the right subtree. Here's the whole function:

```
(defun grow-tree (x tree)
    (cond
      ( (null tree) (make-tree x NIL NIL) )
      ( (= x (value tree)) tree)
      ( ( < x (value tree) ) (make-tree
                                (value tree)
                                (grow-tree x (left-
                                      subtree tree)
                                (right-subtree tree) )
          )
      ( T  (make-tree
                (value tree)
                (left-subtree tree)
                (grow-tree x (right-subtree tree) ) )
          )
      )
)
```

Try this function out with things like:

(setq tree NIL)	returns	NIL
(setq tree (grow-tree 8 tree))		(8 NIL NIL)
(setq tree (grow-tree 4 tree))		(8 (4 NIL NIL) NIL)
(setq tree (grow-tree 10 tree))		(8 (4 NIL NIL) (10 NIL NIL))
(setq tree (grow-tree 2 tree))		(8 (4 (2 NIL NIL) NIL)
		(10 NIL NIL))

You can see the tree being built as list structures.

Searching the Tree

Here we have four conditions to consider. The tree could be empty, its value could be equal to the target (x), the target could lie in the left subtree (if it is less than the value of the tree) or it could lie in the right subtree. Having stated these conditions, the function more or less writes itself:

```
(defun search (x tree)
    (cond
        ( (null tree) NIL)
        ( (= x (value tree) ) T)
        ( (< x (value tree) ) (search x (left-
                      subtree tree) ) )
        ( T (search x (right-subtree tree) ) )
    )
)
```

In practice, of course, we are unlikely to wish to build trees consisting solely of numbers. Certainly the search may take place on a number, such as a record key. If such a key is guaranteed to be the head of a list representing the record, few changes are needed to the tree growing functions. For example, instead of:

```
(= x (value tree) )
```

we would have:

```
(= (head x) (value tree) )
```

where value is now the head of a list representing the root rather than the root itself.

However, this extension leads to an apparent problem with **search**. To be useful, **search** must return the record details, rather than, as now, merely indicate its presence. Since **search** is a recursive function that depends on the fact that it returns T or NIL, what will happen if we make it return a list? Fortunately Lisp sees any non-NIL object as T when it is the argument of a predicate, so it's quite legitimate to replace the (returned) T by (tail x) for instance.

Stacks

Another data structure we shall need later is the stack. Effectively, this is a vector whose top element only can be accessed and to which data can be added

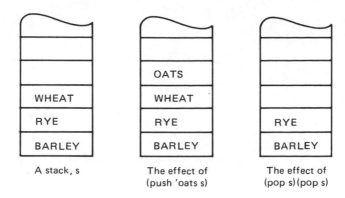

FIGURE 12. Stack operation.

only immediately above this element. We talk about *pushing* data on to a stack and *popping* data off it (see Figure 12).

Stacks are extremely useful for describing the state of a function for an interpreter during the execution of a program. For example, when a function is called, the actual parameters to be manipulated may be pushed on to a stack for easy access by the function. More important, the place to return to once the function is left (the *return address*) is pushed on to a stack. If the function subsequently calls itself, the new return address is pushed on to the stack so that the old one is not only not destroyed, but will be the *second* one to which a return is made, as it should be. It is this mechanism that supports recursive programming.

Common Lisp implements the functions **push** and **pop** directly.

push

The general form of this function is:

```
(push object place)
```

'object' is any Lisp object and 'place' identifies where the **push** should take place. So:

```
(setf y '(a b c) )
(push 3 y)
```

will return:

```
(3 A B C)
```

but:

```
(push 3 '(a b c) )
```

will generate an error message, because '(a b c) is not a place.

Now try:

```
(push 8 (tail y) )
```

You'll see:

>   (8 A B C)

which seems OK because the tail of *y* is (A B C), since '3' is now its head. However, evaluating y will show it to be:

>   (3 8 A B C)

So '8' has been *pushed* on to the tail (and that's what **push** returned) but *y* itself has been altered since it now has the new tail (8 A B C). This isn't too surprising since it's obvious that **push** must have the side effect of altering the stack, but it's important to keep it in mind. Functions with side effects are always the most prone to bugs.

pop

This function takes just one argument, a place to **pop** from. So:

>   (pop y)

will return 3,

>   (pop y) again

will return 8, and y will now be (A B C).
   Again, sneaky code like:

>   (pop (head (tail y))

is legal (and, in this case, will return B, leaving *y* as (A C)) but is not generally desirable, partly because of the side effects problem mentioned earlier and partly because the rules for handling stacks are now being broken. If this turns out to be necessary, a sensible question would be "Why wasn't a vector used instead of a stack?"

Exercises 12

12.1 The **modify-record** function is just one of any number that would be required for a working database. For example, you'd also need **append**, **delete** and **search**. Write versions of these functions.

12.2 Link these functions using **case** to create a simple menu-driven database manager.

Answers

12.1
```
( defun fappend (newrecord)
    (with-open-file (in (merge-pathnames
                            "data.old"))
        (with-open-file (out (merge-pathnames
                                "data.new")
                            :direction :output
```

```
                                            :if-exists :error
                                              )
                          ( loop
                              ( setq record
                                   (read in NIL NIL ) )
                              ( if record
                                   (format out "~A~%" record)
                                   (format out "~A~%"
                                                newrecord)
                              )
                          )
                      )
                  )
( defun fdelete (unrecord)
          (with-open-file (in (merge-pathnames
                               "data.old"))
             (with-open-file (out (merge-pathnames
                                   "data.new")
                          :direction :output
                          :if-exists :error
                          )
                ( loop
                    (setq record
                             (read in NIL NIL) )
                    ( if record
                        ( unless
                            (equal record
                                   unrecord)
                            (format out "~A~%"
                                      record)
                        )
                        (return)
                    )
                )
             )
          )
  )
( defun fsearch(target)
      (with-open-file (in (merge-pathnames
                          "data.old") )
          ( loop
              ( setq record (read in NIL NIL) )
              ( if record
                  ( report record target )
                  ( return )
              )
          )
      )
  )
( defun report (record target)
      ( dolist (field record)
          ( if (equal field target)
              (format T "~%~A" record)
          )
      )
  )
```

```
12.2    ( defun menu()
            (format T "~%DATABASE MANAGER~%")
            (format T "~%Options are")
            (format T "~%1. Modify record")
            (format T "~%2. Append record")
            (format T "~%3. Delete record")
            (format T "~%4. Search database")
            (format T "~%5. Quit")
            (format T "~%Enter option")
            (read)
        )
        ( defun dbms()
            ( loop
                (case (menu)
                        (1 (getmodify))
                        (2 (getappend))
                        (3 (getdelete))
                        (4 (getsearch))
                        (5 (return))
                )
            )
        )
        ( defun getmodify()
            (format T "~%Modify which record?")
            (setq target (read) )
            (format T "~%Enter revision")
            (setq revision (read) )
            (modify-record target revision)
        )
        ( defun getappend()
            (format T "~%Enter record to append")
            (fappend (read) )
        )
        ( defun getdelete()
            (format T "~%Enter record to delete")
            (fdelete (read) )
        )
        ( defun getsearch()
            (format T "~%Enter required field")
            (fsearch (read) )
        )
```

· 13 ·

Arrays, Strings and Structures

For some minutes Alice stood without speaking, looking out in all directions over the country—and a most curious country it was. There were a number of tiny little brooks running straight across it from side to side, and the ground between was divided up into squares by a number of little green hedges, that reached from brook to brook.

Through the Looking-Glass

We have not yet exhausted Lisp's internal data types. In this chapter, I'll introduce a few more. First:

Arrays

Lisp arrays have much the same uses and characteristics as arrays in other languages, so I shall not spend long on them. The Common Lisp definition specifies that implementations must allow for at least seven-dimensional arrays, but I'll restrict this discussion to vectors (i.e. one-dimensional arrays) to begin with. An array is declared using the function **make-array** thus:

```
(setq a (make-array 5) )
```

This will declare an array called *a* to be of length five. We can look at its contents with the function **aref**:

```
(aref a 3)
```

for example, returns element 3 of *a*. If you try this, you'll see it's NIL indicating that **make-array** has initialized the elements of *a*.

```
(aref a 0)
```

also returns NIL, but:

```
(aref a 5)
```

invokes an error message such as "Index out of range". Thus the array has five elements, indexed 0 to 4.

   make-array has a number of keyword arguments, the most useful of which is :initial-contents. This allows a set of values to be plugged into the array to start with. For instance:

```
(setq discount (make-array 4 :initial-contents
'(0 5 7 12) ) )
```

sets up an array called 'discount' containing the values 0, 5, 7 and 12.

```
(aref discount 2)
```

will now yield 7. We have, of course, done nothing that could not have been done using a list, but the index referencing has been made easier for us.

Changing an Array Element

Suppose that the highest discount value changes from 12 to 15. We need a way of saying "Set element 3 of *discount* to 15". This is another situation in which we can use **setf**. Since **aref** provides positional information in the context of an array we can write:

```
(setf (aref discount 3) 15)
```

A subsequent call to **aref**:

```
(aref discount 3)
```

will now give 15.

Multidimensional Arrays

The dimension argument to **make-array** is, in general, a list. So a two-dimensional array might be declared as:

```
(setq two-d (make-array '(4 3) ) )
```

If initial contents are to be set up, the last element of this list determines the length of the innermost initialization list. In other words, we think about *two-d* as containing a list of four lists of length 3 rather than three lists of length 4. For instance:

```
(setq two-d (make-array '(4 3) :initial-contents
             '(
                        ( 1  2  3 )
                        ( 2  4  6 )
                        ( 3  6  9 )
                        ( 4  8  12 )
                   )
              )
)
```

Strings

To all intents and purposes, a string is merely a vector whose elements are characters and functions like **aref** and **setf** can be used on them in the usual way. However, there are a number of string handling functions that make such manipulations somewhat more straightforward.

char

The function **char** has the form:

```
( char string index )
```

For instance:

```
(char "hotdog" 0)
```

will return 'h' (the zeroth element of the vector), and:

```
(char "hotdog" 3)
```

will return 'd'. Since these are characters, though, they will appear as #\h and #\d respectively.

You can use **setf** with **char** to replace a character in a string:

```
(setq x "hotdog")
(setf (char x 1) #\u)
```

will return:

```
#\u
```

but the value of x is now "hutdog".

string=

This function returns T if its two strings arguments are identical. For instance:

```
(string= "hotdog" "hotdog")
```

returns T, but:

```
(string= "hotdog" "Hotdog")
```

returns NIL.

The function **string-equal** can be used if you want a case-insensitive comparison (i.e. **string-equal** would return T in the above example). Both functions are sensitive to white space, so that both see "hotdog" as distinct from "hot dog".

string<

This function returns NIL if its first argument would lie alphabetically after its second. Thus:

```
(string< "baker" "backer")
```

will return NIL.

If the first string *is* less than the second, it returns the index to the first different character. So:

```
(string< "backer" "baker")
```

returns 2:

Other comparator functions are **string/=** (strings not equal), **string<=** (strings less than or equal), and with similarly obvious meanings, **string>** and **string>=**.

Substrings

All these comparator functions can have four keyword arguments :start1, :end1, :start2 and :end2. These define the first and last indexes of the strings under test. Their default values are the beginning and end of the complete arguments, but, if they are specified, substrings can be examined. For example:

```
(string= "barndance" "rnd" :start1 2 :end1 5)
```

returns T. Notice that the index of 'r' in "barndance" is 2 (hence the value of :start1) but 5 is the index of 'a' which is one past the last character in the substring. Thus :end1 − :start1 is the *length* of the substring.

String Manipulation Functions

As a rule, it's easiest to view a string as a vector and simply use the array handling functions already described to mangle a string in whatever way seems convenient. There are, however, some string specific functions that can be quite useful. The following examples serve to introduce some of them and illustrate their uses at the same time:

```
(string-upcase "lower case") returns "LOWER CASE"
(string-downcase "UPPER CASE") returns "upper case"
(string-capitalize "lower case") returns "Lower Case"
```

All the above allow the usual substring keyword arguments.

Structures

Many modern languages allow the user to define his own data types of arbitrary complexity. For example, Pascal uses the concept of a record and C has structures. Neither mechanism gives any new power to the language in question. What it does is to provide a more natural way of referring to data and, by implication, sources of error are reduced. A date is a rather simple example. We could represent it as a six-digit integer, say, 070987. But does this mean July 9 (American standard) or 7th September (English fashion)? We could expand it into a list (07 09 87), which does not solve the ordering problem but at least allows direct access to the individual elements.

A much better solution is to use a structure.

defstruct

The function **defstruct** allows us to describe the features of a data structure for the Lisp interpreter. As we shall see, it does much more besides, but we'll restrict our investigations to this aspect of its use for the moment. This will describe the idea of a date:

```
(defstruct date
                day
                month
                year
)
```

Now let's define a particular instance of a date:

```
(setq birth-date (make-date) )
```

This returns:

```
#S(DATE DAY NIL MONTH NIL YEAR NIL)
```

So the call to defstruct has created a new function called **make-date** which builds a structure of type date. Since I have entered no values for the fields of birth-date, they are set to NIL. However, we can use the field names as keyword arguments to **make-date**:

```
(setq christmas-day (make-date
                          :month 12
                          :day 25
                   )
)
```

This returns:

```
#S(DATE DAY 25 MONTH 12 YEAR NIL)
```

We can also alter a field using **setf**:

```
(setf (date-year christmas-day) 1989)
```

christmas-day is now expressed as:

```
#S(DATE DAY 25 MONTH 12 YEAR 1989)
```

It may by now have occurred to you that you've seen the #S notation before, in the context of file pathnames. This is no accident; pathnames are themselves structures.

What defstruct Does

We can now summarize the tasks that **defstruct** carries out. First, it defines a constructor function called **make-struc** (where struc is the name of the structure). Second, it defines access functions for each field in the structure. These are **date-day**, **date-month** and **date-year** in my example. Each takes a single argument which is an object of the specified type. So, for instance, (date-day christmas-day) will return 25. Additionally, these access functions will work with **setf** to allow the editing of individual fields. Third, a predicate **struc-p** is defined which will return T if its argument is a structure of the given type. Thus (date-p birth-date) will return T, for example.

There are other actions which I shall omit from this discussion. Also there is a range of keyword arguments to **defstruct**. Again, I want to limit this review to just one of them, namely :include. This allows the inclusion of a structure inside another one. For example a book could be described like this:

```
(defstruct (book (:include date) ) title author)
```

A call to **make-book** returns:

```
#S(BOOK DAY NIL MONTH NIL YEAR NIL TITLE NIL AUTHOR NIL)
```

showing that the date information has been included in the structure definition. Note carefully the form of this definition. The :include option is a list containing the include keyword and an existing **defstruct** definition and this must itself form a list with the structure being defined. Only one :include option in a **defstruct** is legal.

Inheritance

Actually, that's a slightly unusual way to use the :include option. More likely, we're trying to expand an existing definition in some fairly marginal way so we can think of the new definition *inheriting* all of the features of the old one and adding a few more. Let's suppose we have a definition of the concept 'jacket':

```
(defstruct jacket size material price)
```

and we now want one for 'overcoat'. We might argue that a jacket is a kind of overcoat but it would be useful to know about its thermal characteristics:

```
(defstruct (overcoat (:include jacket) ) insulation)
```

Now we can say:

```
(setq cia-special (make-overcoat :material 'gabardine
                                 :price    147
                                 :insulation 'poor
                 )
)
```

and:

```
(setq kgb-issue (make-overcoat :material 'wool
                               :insulation 'good
                               :size 'large
                 )
)
```

Obviously we can write:

```
(overcoat-material cia-special)
```

and expect the response GABARDINE, but because (according to this definition) a jacket is a special case of an overcoat we can *also* write:

```
(jacket-material cia-special)
```

with the same effect. Of course:

```
(jacket-insulation kgb-issue)
```

will lead to an error message because insulation characteristics are not defined for jackets.

Exercises 13

13.1 A 3×3 matrix can be represented by the structure **rmatrix** which represents it as a list of three rows, each of which is itself a list of three numbers. For example, the matrix

```
1 2 3
4 5 6
7 8 9
```

becomes

```
( (1 2 3) (4 5 6) (7 8 9) )
```

Define such a structure and set up the above matrix. Then write a function addmx(mat1 mat2) to add two rmatrices, putting the result in an rmatrix sum. You may assume that mat1, mat2 and sum have already been set up as rmatrix structures.

13.2 Using the above structure, matrix multiplication is less straightforward, because it requires the *columns* of the second matrix. Define a new structure cmatrix which represents a matrix as a list of its columns. Write a function rtoc(matrix) which takes a 3×3 matrix in rmatrix format and produces a corresponding cmatrix. Criticize the result.

Answers

13.1   (defstruct rmatrix
                row1
                row2
                row3
)
        (setq mat1 (make-rmatrix
                        :row1 '(1 2 3)
                        :row2 '(4 5 6)
                        :row3 '(7 8 9)
)
)
        (defun addmx(mat1 mat2)
            (setq (row1 sum) (mapcar #'+ (row1 mat1)(row1
                                        mat2)))
            (setq (row2 sum) (mapcar #'+ (row2 mat1)(row2
                                        mat2)))
            (setq (row3 sum) (mapcar #'+ (row3 mat1)(row3
                                        mat2)))
)

13.2   (defstruct cmatrix
                    col1
                    col2
                    col3
)
        (defun rtoc(rmat cmat)
            (setq(col1 cmat)(cons(cons(head(row1 rmat))
                (head(row2 rmat)))(head(row3 rmat))))
            (setq(col2 cmat)(cons(cons(head(tail(row1
                                        rmat)))
                (head(tail(row2 rmat))))(head(tail(row3
                                        rmat)))))
            (setq(col3 cmat)
            (cons(cons(head(tail(tail(row1 rmat))))
                (head(tail(tail(row2 rmat)))))
                (head(tail(tail(row3 rmat)))))))
)

The above code is not exactly elegant, but it does do the job. It strongly suggests that we haven't chosen a particularly good structure for matrices. Indeed, a two-dimensional array would be much more appropriate. Naturally.

· 14 ·

A Pot-Pourri of Features

"It began with blotting-paper," the Knight answered with a groan.
"That wouldn't be very nice, I'm afraid—"
"Not very nice alone," he interrupted, quite eagerly: "but you've no idea what a difference it makes, mixing it with other things—such as gunpowder and sealing wax."

Through the Looking-Glass

As we have now seen, Common Lisp has a range and power exceeded by no other popular language. These very features, however, put the novice programmer in a quandary. How best should a particular function be used? What optional keyword arguments are there that might simplify the code? Is there a more appropriate function anyway? Even the experienced programmer can sometimes feel like a child in a toy supermarket—simply spoilt for choice.

I have, to maintain the analogy, deliberately kept the upper shelves from view so far, occasionally lifting the covers to reveal briefly a gleaming fire engine or sophisticated train set. In truth, it is not the function of this book to do more than this, but I feel that it is at least desirable to expand some topics a little, revise some misconceptions that I have introduced (deliberately!) and point the way towards further investigations with your system manual and other texts.

Functions, Macros and Special Forms

First, I must come clean on the subject of Lisp functions. I have called all Lisp forms that evaluate with zero or more arguments *functions*. In the strictly mathematical sense (provided there are no side effects) this is true enough. But in practice there are considerations that require certain 'functions' to be handled differently. Recall that in Chapter 12 I discussed briefly the way in which a stack is brought into existence for every function call and then destroyed on exit. This is clearly time consuming, so that if a function is to be called frequently, the delays caused may be unacceptable. An alternative is to expand the call into the code that would be called if it were a function. The code is now in-line and there is no need for sophisticated communication mechanisms. This is what is meant by a macro. Examples of macros (that I have already misdescribed as functions) are **push** and **pop**.

There is a third category of apparent 'functions'. These are the *special forms*. As a rule, they are control constructs with some unusual syntactic features. Examples are **if** and **let**.

In fact, when the evaluator is given a list, it examines its head and tries to match it to a special form, a macro and a function in that order.

defmacro

We have managed fine without this knowledge so far and it does not appear to affect the applications programmer much. However, it is possible to define your own macros and, in doing so, save significant processing time. For example, I defined **head** and **tail** as functions in Chapter 2 to relieve us of the burden of having to interpret **car** and **cdr**. A better alternative would have been to define them as macros, since each reference to **head** would then be replaced by **car** rather than initiating an expensive function call. Here's how it's done:

```
(defmacro head (x)
      (list 'car x)
)
(defmacro tail (x)
      (list 'cdr x)
)
```

The form of **defmacro** is similar to that of **defun** in that it begins with the macro name and a list of arguments (here just *x*). The body of the macro differs, however, in that it is not a set of actions to take, but a piece of replacement text.

Thus we are saying here, "On encountering a list consisting of **head** with one argument, replace it with a list consisting of the atom **car** (hence the quote) and the argument".

macroexpand

The function **macroexpand** is what Lisp itself uses to perform the macro expansion, so we can use it to check that our macro does its job properly:

```
(macroexpand '(head test) )
```

This returns:

```
(CAR TEST)
T
```

(CAR TEST) is what we expected, but the T is news. In fact, it indicates that an expansion *was* necessary, but the important point is that this function has returned *two* values. I shall return to this point later.

apply and funcall

I suggested earlier that the user need not be aware whether a form is a function or a macro unless he is interested in the efficiency of the code. That is not quite true. There are two useful functions, **apply** and **funcall**, which take as one argument a function, but will not allow this to be replaced by a macro.

Here's a rather trivial use of **apply**:

```
(setq x '+)
(apply x '(1 2 3) )
```

which returns:

```
6
```

Evidently, **apply** has evaluated its first argument, found it to be a function, and applied it to the list which is its second argument. **funcall** works the same way but expects a sequence of arguments rather than a list:

```
(funcall x 1 2 3)
```

In fact, the above example of **apply** can be directly useful because it allows functions that expect sequences of arguments to operate on lists. However, there are more interesting uses for these two functions.

For example, suppose that we are engaged in evaluating arithmetic and geometric means of lists. In the first case we must add the list elements and in the second we need to multiply them. So we write two simple recursive functions:

```
(defun sum (x)
    (cond
        ( (null x) NIL)
        ( (null (tail x) ) (head x) )
        (T (+ (head x) (sum (tail x) ) ) ) )
    )
)
```

and:

```
(defun product (x)
      (cond
            ( (null x) NIL)
            ( (null (tail x) ) (head x) )
            (T (* (head x) (product (tail x) ) ) )
        )
    )
```

Of course, we see straightaway that these functions are identical except for the single instance of the functions '+' and '*'. So we could write a single function, **sigma**, to which we pass the list to be operated on and the operator function to be used:

```
(defun sigma (x op)
    (cond
          ( (null x ) NIL)
          ( (null (tail x) ) (head x) )
          (T (funcall op (head x)(sigma (tail x ) op)))
      )
)
```

More About Function Arguments

It may have struck you as odd that there exist Lisp primitives that can take indefinitely many arguments and some that take keyword arguments, but that **defun** appears to require an explicitly defined and ordered list of arguments for a function definition. In fact, this is because I have simply not told you enough about **defun**.

Undefined Numbers of Arguments

We already know that functions like + take indefinitely many arguments, so it must be possible to do the same for user-defined functions. We do it by including the parameter &rest in the argument list like this:

```
(defun name (a b c &rest d)
        (. . . .)
    )
```

There are then three ordered formal parameters a, b and c to the function **name**. These may be followed be any number (including zero) of other parameters, collectively called d.

   Here's a useful example. There's a function called **load** that will pull a named file from disk thus:

```
(load "filename")
```

Often, at system startup, you will want to load a series of files—standard macros, debugging tools, your current work file and so on. Using **load** would be annoying because it only takes one argument. Let's define a function **getfiles** to do the operation in one go:

```
(defun getfiles (&rest files)
      (mapcar #'load files)
  )
```

This just accepts indefinitely many arguments called files and then maps the **load** function on to each of them, so we can write:

```
(getfiles "my_macros" "step" "dribble" "work_file")
```

for instance.

Optional Arguments

It's also possible to have arguments that may or may not be present. If they are not, they can be given default values. The mechanism is to use the parameter &optional in a similar manner to &rest.

Let's suppose we have lists that normally represent binary integers and we want a function called **convert** to return the denary equivalent. In principle it's easy—simply multiply the head of the list by 2, add on the next digit (the head of the tail), multiply by 2 again and so on. Since the same algorithm works for any base, just by changing the multiplier, it would be nice to have this as an optional argument, defaulting to 2. Here's one solution:

```
(defun convert (x &optional (radix 2) )
    (setq result 0)
    (dolist
         (digit x result)
         (setq result (+ digit (* result radix) ) )
    )
)
```

You can call this with:

```
(convert '(1 0 1 1 1) )
```

to get 23, or

```
(convert '(1 0 1 1 1) 3)
```

to get 94.

This is a nice use for **dolist**, but *result* is a free variable and consequently dangerous. It's interesting to consider the recursive equivalent:

```
(defun convert (x &optional (radix 2) )
    (cond
       ( (null x) NIL)
       ( (null (tail x) ) (head x) )
       (T (+ (head x)
             (* radix (convert (tail x) radix) ) ) )
    )
)
```

A cursory glance at this function shows that it handles the list back to front because the final element added is the head! This isn't a real problem because there is a built-in *reverse* function that we could call first. It would be trivial to write anyway. The important point about this function is the form of the recursive call to **convert**. The *radix* argument is no longer optional! Of course, there is no *need* for it to be, because by the time the code is executed, *radix* has either defaulted to 2 or been explicitly set. However, if you *do* declare it as optional, the interpreter will claim it has found an unbound variable, which is mildly confusing.

Keyword Arguments

I have already introduced the idea of a keyword argument and pointed out that its advantage is that the user needs to remember no specific order of arguments when using a function. Let's now see how to write such functions. The general form is:

```
(defun name (&key x y)
     (. . . .)
)
```

Now **name** is a function having two keyword arguments that can be called with:

```
(name :x 7 :y 3)
```

or

```
(name :y 3 :x 7)
```

with identical results. Let's write a function **lookup** that examines a list for the presence of a particular atom. Conventionally, this could be called with:

```
(lookup g h)
```

and nobody, including the programmer, has the slightest idea whether *g* is being looked for in *h* or vice versa. Using keyword arguments, we can write:

```
(lookup :atom g :list h)
```

Altogether more satisfactory. Here's the code:

```
(defun lookup (&key atom list)
     (cond
           ( (null list ) NIL)
           ( (eq (head list) atom) T )
           ( T (lookup :atom atom :list (tail list) ) )
     )
)
```

Simple, elegant and convenient!

Multiple-Valued Functions

When I introduced **macroexpand**, I noted that it returns *two* values. This seems out of keeping with the nature of a functional language (after all, how can a function have two meanings at the same time?) and, in any case, the same effect could be achieved by returning a list. The justification (which I am not entirely happy with) is pragmatic. First, there is an overhead in consing up a list. Second, it is likely that the calling function will only want the head of this list anyway, so it seems wasteful to have to generate repeatedly forms like (head returned-result).

Fortunately, normal functions simply ignore all but the first-mentioned value, so there is nothing to stop you writing:

```
(setq x (macroexpand '(head p) ) )
```

for instance.

If you *do* need the other returned values, the simplest method is to use the function **multiple-value-list** which returns a list of them. For example:

```
(multiple-value-list (macroexpand '(head x) ) )
```

returns:

```
( (CAR X) T)
```

It is, of course, possible to build your own functions that return multiple values, but, as I've already pointed out, it is strictly unnecessary, so I shall not pursue this line of enquiry further.

Packages

I have previously pointed out that real software projects are social activities involving tens or even hundreds of programmers. Unless each member of the team can ensure that his functions and data do not conflict with those of other programmers, the result of their combined labours is almost guaranteed to crash in baffling ways. We have seen some ways of limiting the possible damage, using **let** and **flet**, for instance, but Common Lisp has a much more satisfying solution to the problem. It allows code to be written within a module called a *package*. Each package is completely independent of all others, save one. This is the package LISP, which contains all the primitive definitions, global variables and so on that will be required by all other packages. Try this:

```
*package*
```

The system responds:

```
#<PACKAGE USER>
```

The system variable *package* holds the currently active package, which defaults to USER (or, on some systems, LISP).

Now write:

```
( in-package "TEST" )
```

This returns:

```
#<PACKAGE TEST>
```

In fact, in-package looks for an existing package called TEST to transfer to. In this case it fails, so it creates one first and then enters it.

Now write some trivial function:

```
( defun inc (x)
     ( + x 1 )
)
```

Confirm that it works and return to USER with:

```
( in-package "USER" )
```

(Note that, because the argument of **in-package** is a string, it is case sensitive. Thus the packages USER and user are distinct.)

Now a call such as:

```
( inc 5 )
```

will give an invalid function message. Fair enough; **inc** is restricted to TEST. But it *can* still be accessed. Try:

```
( TEST::inc 5 )
```

This returns 6. In other words, you can tell Lisp that you want a function from another package by preceding it with the package name and *two* colons. This notation is deliberately clumsy to underline the fact that inter-package communication is likely to be a source of unpleasant bugs.

It is also possible to communicate data between packages, but the 'home' package of the data must allow this explicitly. To see how, return to the package TEST and write:

```
( setq v 7 )
```

say. Now, to make *v* available elsewhere, we must deliberately **export** it:

```
( export 'v )
```

Note that it is the *symbol v* that is exported. Back inside USER, we can now write:

```
TEST:v
```

and get the response:

```
7
```

This time, a single colon is used to separate the package name from the variable. Now write:

```
( setq TEST:v (+ 3 TEST:v) )
```

which naturally returns 10. You can easily check that *v* inside TEST is also 10. This is no surprise, because *v* in TEST is not merely equivalent to *TEST:v* everywhere else; they are the *same* variable.

It is possible, but dangerous, to internalize the functions and variables of one package into another, so that the home package name need not be referred to, although I shall not describe the mechanism here. In fact, this is the way the LISP package makes itself available to the user. So it should be possible to replace a reference to a function such as **cons** with its full title LISP::cons as in:

```
( LISP::cons 'a 'b )
```

which returns:

```
( a . b )
```

Parallel and Sequential Assignments

In most computer languages, we expect operations to occur in a sequence defined by the order of the program statements. Indeed, this usually happens in Lisp, either implicitly, or as an explicit **progn**. However, there are some exceptions.

psetq

This function allows a set of assignments to be made in parallel. So, for instance,

```
(psetq x y y x)
```

swaps the contents of *x* and *y*. Ironically, when beginners are introduced to a conventional procedural language, they often make the mistake of assuming a human-like parallel operating model, and so write something like:

```
x := y;
y := x;
```

when asked to write a swap routine. They are confused when it doesn't work. Exactly the reverse confusion can confront the experienced programmer working in Lisp for the first time . . .

let*

When I introduced **let**, I omitted to mention that it makes its variable assignments in parallel, like **psetq**. Normally, this makes no difference, *unless* you want to assign a value to a variable that has been previously assigned in the same **let**. Because the operations are performed in parallel, the phrase 'previously assigned' is misleading. It refers only to the order of presentation of the code, not to the order of execution. If you do want to perform a *sequence* of assignments, you have to use **let***.

Comments

You've probably noticed that none of the code so far presented in this book has been commented. This is because each function has been quite short and has been described in detail in the text. In practice, of course, the programmer's mechanism for documenting the code is to sprinkle comments throughout it. A Lisp comment is initiated with a semicolon and terminated with a new line. From chapter 16 onwards, much of the code is commented in this way. A word of warning though: comments should be *useful*. I've seen a line like:

```
(setq x 0) ;initialize x to zero
```

in a professional programmer's code. Honest!

Exercises 14

14.1 In about 1220, Leonardo of Pisa came up with an interesting problem
about rabbits. If a breeding pair produces one new pair of offspring once a
month and it takes one month for the new pairs to become productive, and
you start with one pair—how does the population grow? (For simplicity,
we assume exactly regular production each month and that every pair
consists of one male and one female.) Write a function rabbit(n) which
calculates the total number of rabbits after n months.

Answers

14.1   ```
(defun rabbit(n)
     (do
          (
                    (m 1 (+ 1 m))
                    (b 1 (+ b i))
                    (i 0 b)
)
          ((= m n) (+ b i))
)
)
```

This needs a little explanation. The variables $m,b,i$ contain the month, the
number of breeding pairs and the number of immature pairs. At the next stage $m$
must change to $m+1$; $b$ becomes $b+i$ because the immature pairs are now able to
breed; and $i$ becomes $b$ because each breeding pair produces a new immature
pair.

The point to notice is that **do**, like **let**, makes these changes in parallel, so the
code can take the above direct form. The total number of rabbits is $b+i$.

Incidentally, the answers should look suspiciously familiar. You wrote an
equivalent function in a quite different way a few chapters ago. Which one?
```

· 15 ·

Debugging Techniques

"That is not said right," said the Caterpillar.

"Not quite right, I'm afraid," said Alice, timidly: "some of the words have got altered."

"It is wrong from beginning to end," said the Caterpillar, decidedly.

Alice's Adventures in Wonderland

The fact that much Lisp code is recursive can make debugging even more of a headache than is usually the case. In an ideal world, full of clear headed programmers, and programs built from nice little functions, each of which is doing a limited and precisely defined job, nothing can, of course, go wrong, go wrong, go wrong . . .

But this isn't an ideal world. Naturally, functions should be small and carefully tested (I have a maxim: "Design top-down—debug bottom-up") but it's always the three line function that can't possibly have anything wrong with it that obstinately refuses to do what clearly it was designed to. That is when programming becomes exasperating and every programmer would love to have the mnemonic opcode DWIT (Do What I'm Thinking). And that's precisely the problem: the mismatch between what the programmer has written and what he (or she) thinks is there. Debugging is all about finding clues to this mismatch, seeking out, if you will, the details of the system's 'thought' processes.

Using format

Where to start? Perhaps the simplest thing to do is to include a **format** call in a function under test to look at the way variables are changing during execution. Recall, by way of example, the **power** function of Chapter 4. I'll rewrite it slightly to introduce a bug and insert a **format** call at the beginning:

```
( defun power ( x n )
        ( format T "~%x is ~a n is ~a" x n )
        ( cond
                ( (zerop n) 1 )
                ( T (* x (power x (- 1 n) ) ) ) )
        )
)
```

Evaluating (power 3 4) gives:

```
x is 3 n is 4
x is 3 n is -3
x is 3 n is 4
x is 3 n is -3
```

and so on until the stack overflows. It's immediately clear that n is not decrementing correctly. In fact, of course, the arguments to '$-$' are the wrong way round.

break

Unfortunately, the figures flash before your eyes at an alarming rate and, of course, you can't look at any other intermediate results that occur to you. The function **break** allows you to think about the problem one loop at a time, and at your own pace. It has a similar form to **format**, except that it does not require a stream argument, so that it would appear in the above example as:

```
( break "~%x is ~a n is ~a" x n )
```

This time, evaluating **power** gives something like:

```
Breaking:
        x is 3 n is 4
Starting listener BREAK
>>
```

You can now examine or reset any variables you like and then resume execution with 'cont'. So the whole exchange might go:

```
Breaking:
      x is 3 n is 4
Starting listener BREAK
>>(setq n 1)
1
>>cont
Breaking:
x is 4 n is 0
Starting listener BREAK
>>
```

and so on.

Unfortunately, the precise action of **break** is implementation dependent so the messages may differ a little and the 'cont' command may be different; but you get the general idea.

The Stepper

The stepper allows us to look at the result of evaluating a function, form by form. Suppose that we wish to do this on the tree searching function of Chapter 12. We might type:

```
( step ( search 3 '(8 NIL NIL) ) )
```

So **search** is looking for 3 in a tree consisting only of the root 8. The stepper shows the form to be evaluated first:

```
1 → (SEARCH 3 (QUOTE (8 NIL NIL)))
:
```

The '1' indicates the level of evaluation and the '→' shows that this form is about to be evaluated. The colon prompt requests a command. A list of available commands can usually be generated by hitting '?'. We shall consider only one here, which, on my system, is 'n' for 'next'. This gives:

```
2 → 3
```

showing that 3 is about to be evaluated. Then:

```
2 ← 3 3
```

tells us that '3' is evaluated (←) and the result is (unsurprisingly) 3. The sequence continues:

```
2 → (QUOTE (8 NIL NIL))
2 ← (QUOTE (8 NIL NIL)) (8 NIL NIL)
2 → (COND ((NULL TREE) NIL)((= X #) T)((<X #)(SEARCH X
#))..)
3 → (NULL TREE)
4 → TREE
4 ← TREE (8 NIL NIL)
3 ← (NULL TREE) NIL
```

And so on, and so on. When you're really stuck, this can be a useful function, but there is an evident danger that the stepper gives you so much information that you can lose the thread of what is going on. There are usually ways to limit how much the stepper tells you, but it takes some practice to decide exactly how much (or how little) you really need to know.

trace

Often, it's adequate just to know how frequently a function is called and what its arguments and returned values are. Try this:

```
( trace search )
```

Now evaluate:

```
( search 3 '( 8 ( 3 NIL NIL ) NIL ))
```

You'll get a display like:

```
TRACE: (1) Entering SEARCH arglist = (3 (8 (3 NIL NIL)
NIL ))
TRACE: (2) Entering SEARCH arglist = (3 (3 NIL NIL))
TRACE: (2) Exiting SEARCH value(s) = T
TRACE: (1) Exiting SEARCH value(s) = T
T
```

Now you can see the recursion level very easily, indicated by the number in brackets. You can also see how the arguments change and watch the recursion 'unwind'. The trace is turned off with:

```
( untrace search )
```

Incidentally, **trace** will take indefinitely many arguments as in:

```
( trace search power dec )
```

and may do many cleverer things, but these are implementation dependent.

apropos

A particularly pretty little function for examining groups of related functions and variables is **apropos**. This takes a string argument which it attempts to match with the text currently available to the interpreter. Thus, assuming you have our tree handling functions loaded:

```
( apropos "TREE" )
```

might elicit a response like:

```
tree
        internal symbol in #<package USER>
        Value is undefined
        Function is undefined
        No properties
        ----------------------------------------------------
```

```
grow-tree
        internal symbol in #<package USER>
        Value is undefined
        Function is
              an interpreted function
                    arglist: ( x tree )
        No properties
        ------------------------------------------------
tree-equal
        external symbol in #<package LISP>
        Value is undefined
        Function is
              a compiled function
        No properties
        ------------------------------------------------
    etc, etc.
```

Now, what is interesting here is that **apropos** finds the text to match anywhere at all, so, as you can see, it finds a function called **tree-equal** in the LISP package. Thus, quite apart from confirming for you that you do indeed have the functions you think you defined, **apropos** can sometimes save you from reinventing the wheel by drawing your attention to a function you didn't know existed. Just occasionally, debugging becomes the art of throwing away a bugged function and replacing it with one that was already there!

time

Finally, I want to mention a function that isn't really a debugging tool at all, but rather, an optimizing one. This is **time**, which tells you how long a function takes to execute and usually adds other information as well, such as the number of conses that occurred. To examine **search** we might write:

```
( time (search 3 '(8 (3 NIL NIL) NIL )))
```

Precisely how the system responds is implementation dependent, but it will certainly include the evaluation time. This lets you compare different approaches to a problem very easily.

· 16 ·
Object-Oriented Programming

*'Be what you seem to be'—or, if you'd like it put more simply—
'Never imagine yourself not to be otherwise than what it might appear to
others that what you were or might have been was not otherwise than
what you had been would have appeared to them to be otherwise.'*

Alice's Adventures in Wonderland

The traditional view of software systems is that they consist of the data that
represents some information and a set of procedures that manipulates the data.
However, this doesn't always work . . . For instance, if you are given the
instruction

    subtract 38 from 16,

then the answer will depend on the context. If the 16 represents your bank
balance, what happens depends on your bank manager. If he won't give you an

overdraft, the result remains 16 but you don't get the 38. If the 16 is degrees Celsius, then the answer is −22. If you're playing darts, the answer is 16, and you've lost the rest of your turn.

An alternative philosophy would be to create a collection of techniques, which collectively amount to the concept 'subtract' in all relevant contexts. The combination of the concepts 'subtract' and 'bank balance' would then lead to a different result from the combination 'subtract' and 'dartboard'. The aim of this chapter is to describe just such a philosophy, known as *object-oriented programming*.

objects

An object-oriented system has a single entity—the *object*. There are two components to an object: the information that defines it, and a set of *methods* for manipulating that information.

The terminology used in object-oriented programming has not been standardized, but it's generally easy to relate one set of definitions to another. I will base my terminology on Smalltalk, the original object-oriented language.

The object to be manipulated is called the *receiver* of the message. A message comprises a symbolic name (the *selector*) that describes the type of manipulation desired, together with any other objects that take part in the manipulation (the *message arguments*). For example, consider a program controlling windows on a screen. In order to move a window to a new position on the screen, a message conveying instructions along the lines of 'move window to position 20, 30, . . .' must be obeyed.

This requires an object 'window', a selector 'move', and arguments '20, 30, . . .' specifying the window coordinates. The Lisp syntax is:

```
(selector argument1 argument2 argument 3 ...)
```

or in this case

```
(move window 20 30 ...).
```

The set of messages to which an object can respond is its *protocol*. Externally, the user views only the protocol. Internally, the methods are more conventional. Thus a message alone does not determine exactly what will happen; this depends upon the *receiver* of the message as well. Each object therefore has a set of private variables for this purpose. For example, a 'window' object might represent its location and size internally in several different ways. The *private variables* might contain:

1. Four numbers representing the x and y location of the centre, the width, and the height.
2. Two points representing opposite corners of the window.
3. A single rectangle whose location and size are the same as those of the window.

The method that moves the window assumes a particular representation. If the representation changes so does the method, but only the methods within the object need changing.

Classes

Most object-oriented systems distinguish between the description of an object and the object itself. Many similar objects can be described by the same general description called the class.

A *class* is a description of one or more similar objects.
An *instance* is an object described by a particular class.

Each instance contains information that distinguishes it from other instances. This information is held in a subset of the private variables called *instance variables*, which differ in value from instance to instance. For example, the 'window' object could have an instance variable which takes values 1, 2 or 3 corresponding to the three types of representation above.

All instances of a class have the same number of instance variables. Common information shared by all instances are retained in *class variables*.

Inheritance allows for the creation of classes related to other classes. The first class is referred to as the *superclass* and the second the *subclass*. Subclasses may differ from their superclass by:

adding instance variables,
providing new methods for some of the messages understood by the superclass,
providing methods for new messages (not understood by the superclass), or
adding class variables.

The great attraction of the object-oriented philosophy is that the same messages can be used, even if the specification of the object changes. This is possible because an object includes the rules needed to manipulate it: if you change the specification of an object you must of course change these rules appropriately.

Software engineers have been promoting this concept of 'reusability' for many years, but until recently had not formalized it.

It takes four things to make these ideas work:

1. *Information Hiding*. This means that the state of the object is contained in private variables, and localized procedures manipulate the data directly.
2. *Data Abstraction*. Information can only be hidden if data is abstracted. The user views the object as a 'black box' and need have no knowledge of the internal data structures or manipulations required to perform a specific task.
3. *Dynamic Binding*. This means that the data carries with it the necessary information for its manipulation. For example, although 'subtract money' and 'subtract darts score' work in different ways, 'subtract' would be carried out correctly in either case. In the literature, you may see the term 'heterogeneous data environment' used in this context.
4. *Inheritance*. Inheritance lets us define 'generic' objects, and relate individual instances back to the class. New methods and variables can be added if required, but all inherited parameters and methods can be accessed. Multiple inheritance allows for new objects derived from more than one class. Logically, multiple inheritance must be structured to define the dominant inheritance characteristics. For instance the sequence of method searching must be unambiguous.

Objection!

The functions introduced above are not defined in Common Lisp, although several implementations include something similar. However, it's easy to see how the ideas of information hiding, data abstraction, and dynamic binding can be modelled using packages.

We encountered packages in Chapter 14. When we wanted to access the variables and functions defined in a package, we had to include the package name to specify the environment in which the interpreter would search. The two obvious results are that the name of the object (or package) provides us with the necessary linking information and the object hides its contents (variables and functions) from the global Lisp environment.

Also, I've already introduced the idea of inheritance in Chapter 13, in the context of structures. So it wouldn't be hard to put the object-oriented philosophy into practice, even if your version of Lisp didn't include it.

Objection overruled.

Example

To illustrate these ideas, in particular that of inheritance, here is a typical interactive session with added commentary. We assume that the functions **kindof**, **ask**, and **have** have already been written. In fact what follows is based on the Coral Common Lisp implementation, but the precise details are irrelevant.

```
? (setq pet (kindof NIL))
#<Object #169, a generic object>
```

The function **kindof** creates a new container or object into which we can place variables and functions that are appropriate for the object which is named 'pet'. The Lisp interpreter creates the object and provides it with a unique identifier.

```
? (ask pet (have 'owner))
NIL
```

When we wish to access or modify the contents of an object we must identify the object by name and pass to it the request for action, which is called the message. The message (have 'owner) tells the 'pet' object that it should add a variable 'owner' to its contents.

```
? (ask pet (setq owner "Fletcher Christian"))
"Fletcher Christian"
```

In this case we are passing a message to 'pet' which assigns the value "Fletcher Christian" to the variable 'owner'.

```
? (ask pet owner)
"Fletcher Christian"
```

Ask returns the name of the variable within pet, so the response is the value we have assigned to 'owner', namely "Fletcher Christian".

What happens if we try to find the value of the *global* variable 'owner'?

```
? owner
> Error: Unbound variable: OWNER.
> While executing: SYMBOL-VALUE
```

The response shows us that at the global level 'owner' does not exist. It has been created, and therefore exists, only within the object 'pet'. This does not prevent us from also having a global variable called 'owner'. Let's confirm that by setting up such a global variable and assigning it a different value.

```
? (setq owner "Christopher Columbus")
"Christopher Columbus"
? owner
"Christopher Columbus"
? (ask pet owner)
"Fletcher Christian"
```

We have indeed created a global variable 'owner' which can store a completely different value from that within 'pet'. So far so good. Here comes the subtle bit.

Inheritance

In Chapter 13 we found that a new structure can inherit attributes from a previous one, to which we may add extra features as necessary. We didn't have to reinvent the wheel.

We need a form of inheritance which

1. allows attributes to be inherited if they are what we need,
2. allows us to add new attributes if necessary,
3. lets us replace or modify attributes that are incorrect or incomplete.

In the above example the object 'pet' exists within the global Lisp environment and *can inherit attributes* from this environment. Packages alone can't do this. Let's investigate inheritance further:

```
? (setq city "Perth")
"Perth"
? city
"Perth"
```

Within the global environment we have created a new variable 'city' and assigned it a value. What happens if we ask the object 'pet' for the value of 'city'?

```
? (ask pet city)
"Perth"
```

We get the answer "Perth" which was created and assigned at the global level. Inheritance has provided the answer. We send a message to 'pet' asking for the value of 'city'. 'Pet' checks its own variables and doesn't find 'city'. It therefore passes the message to its ancestor, which in this case is the global environment, where an answer "Perth" is found and returned. This explains the 'generic object' response when we created 'pet' in the first place. It was telling us that the immediate ancestor of 'pet' is the global environment.

We can, of course, change the response from 'pet' by sending it a message telling it to assign the variable 'city' a value.

```
? (ask pet (setq city "New York"))
"New York"
? (ask pet city)
"New York"
? city
"New York"
```

An Australian Prime Minister once said "Life wasn't meant to be easy". He was right. Inheritance is not a one way street: if the object does not have the answer then it passes the message to its ancestor. The next interactive segment shows what can happen. The message asks for the variable 'city' to be changed to "New York". The object 'pet' doesn't have its own variable 'city' so it passes the message on, with the result that the global variable is changed whether or not we meant it to be. If we really intend just to change the response of 'pet' we must give it a variable of its own called 'city'.

```
? (ask pet (have 'city))
NIL
? (ask pet (setq city "Perth"))
"Perth"
? (ask pet city)
"Perth"
? city
"New York"
```

It is important to remember that when we wish to change the response of an object to a specific request we must provide the object with its own version.

We have learnt a certain amount about inheritance with only one object derived from the Lisp environment, but we must delve deeper to find out more.

```
? (setq continent "Australia")
"Australia"
? (ask pet continent)
"Australia"
? (setq Joey (kindof pet))
#<Object #170, a #169>
```

We have now created a new object but we have stated that it is a **kindof** 'pet'. This tells Lisp that the new object inherits the characteristics of the object 'pet'. Let's check it out.

```
? (ask Joey owner)
"Fletcher Christian"
```

Joey inherited this response from 'pet' and will do the same for 'city'.

```
? (ask Joey city)
"Perth"
```

What happens if we ask 'Joey' the value of 'continent'? The message is not satisfied by 'Joey' so it is passed to 'pet'. There is no satisfaction here either, so the message passes to the global environment and finds an answer there.

```
? (ask Joey continent)
"Australia"
```

The 'Joey' object can, of course, have its own variables, and these are then local to the object.

```
? (ask Joey (have 'age "Young"))
"Young"
? age
> Error: Unbound variable: AGE.
> While executing: SYMBOL-VALUE
? (ask pet age)
> Error: Unbound variable: AGE.
> While executing: SYMBOL-VALUE
? (ask Joey age)
"Young"
```

Functions

So far I have concentrated on variables and shown how they may be seen as existing within an object or inherited by the object. When I related objects to packages I indicated that functions may also belong to an object. As you might expect, they can be inherited from ancestor objects if necessary. We must inform the Lisp interpreter that the new function belongs to a specific object.

```
? (defobfun (display pet) (sentence)
    (princ "*** ")
    (princ sentence)
    (princ " ***")
    (terpri)
)
```

display

A special version **defobfun** of **defun** provides the facility to add a function to an object. Let's test our new function within the various object environments.

```
? (display "HELLO")
> Error: Undefined function: DISPLAY.
> While executing: EVAL
? (ask pet (display "HELLO"))
*** HELLO ***
NIL
? (ask Joey (display owner))
*** Fletcher Christian ***
NIL
? (ask Joey ( display age))
*** Young ***
NIL
?
```

The function **display** is available to 'pet' and to those objects that inherit from it.

The above example is rather academic. Here is a more practical one. At the beginning of this chapter we mentioned the idea of seeing a screen window as an object. We can now see that object-oriented programming would provide a flexible approach to windows, making it easy to implement them on different systems in a consistent way. The 'windows' class would include all common functions such as **move**, **resize**, **close**, etc. Actual windows on the computer screen would have their own individual characteristics such as size, shape and location. In writing new software we code only those functions that are specific to the new application. All other characteristics are inherited and the general class software is reuseable.

· 17 ·

ABC

"Of course you know your ABC?" said the Red Queen.
"To be sure I do," said Alice.

Through the Looking-Glass

So far we have written isolated functions to illustrate particular features of Lisp. But practical programs are structured sequences of large numbers of functions. To show how a complete system might be written, the last three chapters deal with an interpreter for (a subset of) the language ABC, written in Lisp. ABC is a structured interactive computer language produced by the Centre for Mathematics and Computer Science in Amsterdam. The original versions were written by Lambert Meertens and Leo Guerts around 1976. The third version (known as ABC B) was designed with the aid of Robert Dewar of New York University.

This chapter is mostly about ABC itself, while Chapters 18 and 19 describe the interpreter.

Examples of ABC Code

What does ABC look like as a language? A few examples will illustrate its simplicity and style. Suppose you wish to build a telephone directory. You must create an empty table and then add the numbers to it:

```
ABC> PUT {} IN phone
ABC> PUT 7296 IN phone [ "Jim" ]
ABC> PUT 7248 IN phone [ "Alan" ]
```

Looking up someone's number, or changing it or adding someone else is easy:

```
ABC> WRITE phone [ "Alan" ]
7248
ABC> PUT 2967 IN phone [ "Ann" ]
ABC> WRITE phone
"Alan" 7428 "Ann" 2967 "Jim" 7296
```

Note that the entries are printed in alphabetical order.

What about program control? One way that ABC can handle loop structures is as follows:

```
ABC> PUT 1300 , 0 IN x , c
ABC> WHILE x > 0 : PUT x / 10 , c + 1 IN x , c
ABC> WRITE c
4
```

This begins by setting x = 1300 and c = 0. It then successively divides x by 10 (putting the result back in x) and adds 1 to c. It stops when x becomes zero—that is, smaller than the smallest nonzero floating-point number that can be represented in the machine. The final value of c counts how many divisions by 10 have occurred.

Description of the Language

To keep the length within bounds, our interpreter will implement only a subset of ABC, and we describe that subset.

Data Types. ABC has five: numbers, strings, compound values, lists, and tables. The subset has *integer* numbers, strings, and tables.

Commands. ABC has four commands to manipulate data structures: put, insert, remove, delete. There are two I/O commands: read, write. There are five flow-control commands: if, while, for, select, check. Finally there is a randomizing command: set random.

The subset just has put, write, if, and while.

Definitions. In ABC new commands and functions may be defined, using 'how to'. The subset does not have this facility.

Operators. ABC has the usual arithmetical operators $+, -, *, /, **, =, <>, >, <$, together with some extras such as random, root, min, max, choice. It also has various text operators. The subset implements $+, -, *, /, =, >, <$.

Before We Start . . .

You'll see that the more sophisticated features of ABC are largely missing from the interpreter. (This has the advantage of making the interpreter intelligible.) Those catered for are largely self-explanatory. For this reason we won't discuss the language any further: if you want to know more, see "An Alternative Simple Language and Environment for PCs" by Steven Pemberton, *IEEE Software*, January 1987, pp. 56–64.

In the next two chapters, when we present the interpreter in detail, you'll notice some changes in programming style. For example, we have reverted from **head** and **tail** to the standard **car** and **cdr**. The reason for these changes is that we want you to see what code actually looks like in practice. By now we don't anticipate that cosmetic changes of this kind will cause you any difficulty.

In the same vein, the bracket-pairing format that we have used so far would become very space consuming in a large piece of code, so we shall revert to a more compressed style. Of course, you should bear in mind that the format in which you write code, and the format in which it finally appears, need not be the same. Indeed, you can write the code using as much indentation as you like, and compress the final version using the pretty-printer.

The block structuring in ABC is shown by indentation and is simplified by incorporating a syntax sensitive editor. For simplicity, in the interpreter I've introduced a continuation keyword '→' used at the end of a line to indicate that the block is incomplete. For example,

```
ABC> PUT 0 , 0 IN f , c
ABC> WHILE f<5 : PUT f + 1 , 5 * ( f - 32 ) / 9 IN f , c →
ABC> WRITE f , Fahrenheit , c , Centigrade
```

In ABC, block continuation is part of the function definition structure, and this example is not legal.

ABC Interpreter: Scanner

*She went back to the table, half hoping she might find another key on it,
or at any rate a book of rules.*

Alice's Adventures in Wonderland

An interpreter for any language (including Lisp) must have a read → translate →
execute loop which takes the user's keyboard input and analyses it to determine
what the user wants, translates it into executable form, and finally does the
work. This chapter deals with the read → translate stage; the next handles the
actual execution.

Overall Structure

In this implementation I collect a line of information from the user, and then
pass this to the analyser, which extracts the lexical (or keyword) and syntactic
(or specific pattern) structures of the ABC statement. This information is then
passed to the execution routine, which evaluates the list supplied.

The listing below shows how to implement the overall structure of ABC.
Provided all of the ABC interpreter has been loaded, a session may be started by
evaluating (ABC).

```
; Set up a flag to control the debugging print statements
(setq *mybugs* NIL)
; Set up any initial requirements for the ABC interpreter
(defun initialise ()
(setq *myerrors* NIL)) ; An error-detected flag
(setq mysave NIL); A continuation flag/variable
; If a complete structure is available execute it
(defun execute (analysed-list)
(cond (*myerrors* t)
((null analysed-list) NIL)
(T ; If needed show what was received then "eval" it.
   (cond (*mybugs* (print "EXECUTE") (princ
     analysed-list)))
   (terpri) (eval analysed-list) t) ; return true
))
; Input string is scanned
; Algebraic functions are removed and analysed
; to reduce complexity of the token list
; Lexical analysis of the list is then completed
(defun analyse (input-string)
(cond (*myerrors* t)
   ((string-equal input-string "quit") NIL)
   ; Interpreter has finished
   (T (syntax (reduce-token-list (scanner input-
string))))
))
; This simply provides the read → translate → execute
; loop until quit time
; All symbols must be delimited by a space
; A NIL return from execute finishes the execution
; of the interpreter
(defun ABC ()
(initialise )
; (read-line)NOT NEEDED in CORAL Lisp but required for
; VAX Lisp
(princ "This is the ABC Interpreter")
(loop
   (setq *myerrors* NIL)(terpri)(print "ABC> ")
   (if (not (execute (analyse (read-line))))
     (return "End of the ABC Interpreter"))
))
```

I have defined two global variables here to support the software development
and implementation of the interpreter. Recall that the *variable* notation is
used to emphasize the global nature of a system variable.

The first global variable is *mybugs* which, if set to true, ensures that special
print statements scattered at appropriate places within the software will be
activated and give information about the results of the processing. This is a
simple but effective way of helping the debugging process and will help you
understand the interpretation process.

The second variable is *myerrors* which is used within the software to indicate that certain errors have been detected by the ABC interpreter, and that an appropriate message has been sent to the user. This allows the interpreter to carry on for further input. Common Lisp will, of course, detect other errors and exit to its own debugger. The interpreter environment has been set up so that you may reenter ABC without losing the current status, provided you have not started a new Common Lisp session.

read-line does not allow for typing errors and may cause some frustration for you, but it is the simplest Common Lisp function meeting the requirements. I've found that there are some versions of Common Lisp which may require an extra **read-line** to clear the input before ABC becomes operative.

The Scanner

Any programming language possesses a set of grammatical rules. A statement in the language is just a text string that obeys these rules. To interpret this string I must identify those parts that have meaning as keywords within the language, and those that represent data or new variables.

It's easy to think of the text as a sequence of *tokens*, where a token represents a basic element of the language. For instance, if I enter

```
PUT 129 , 235 IN x , y
```

then I've created a sequence of eight tokens separated by spaces which include two keywords (PUT and IN), two delimiters (both ,), two variables (x and y) and two integers (129 and 235).

The job of recognizing and classifying tokens is called *lexical analysis*, and the part of the interpreter which handles this task is the *scanner*. The scanner replaces the original text by a list of 'token lists', each consisting of a code number followed by any other information that may be useful for the subsequent analysis of the program statement.

If I enter the ABC statement above (and had previously created the variables x and y) then the scanner will return

```
((51 |y| "y")(30)(51 |x| "x")(4)(50 235)(30)(50 129)(6))
```

which needs some explaining. I must have a symbol table to be searched for the tokens, plus some additional information about each token. I have copied this additional information into the token list. The output list is in reverse order when compared with the original string, because I've used stack operations to save each succeeding token list. We may use a list as a stack very easily, as was shown in Chapter 12. When using stacks it is sometimes necessary to check the value on top of the stack—nondestructively. It is easy to write a function **tos** to achieve this:

```
(defun tos (name)
      (if (null name)
          NIL
          (car name)
))
```

All except the definition of **tos** are predefined in Common Lisp, so these definitions are not needed for the interpreter.

Symbol Table

A *symbol table* is required to hold information about each recognizable symbol. I've created a variable called *keytable* which stores a table of token information based on a binary tree. The tokens are the keys used to look into the table. This technique minimizes the search time through a large symbol table: see Chapter 12.

```
(setq *keytable* '((("]" 37) (("/" 56 TRUNCATE)
                    (("+" 55 +) ((")" 57)
((("(" 54) NIL NIL) (("*" 56 *) NIL NIL)) (("," 30) NIL
                    (("-" 55 -) NIL
(("→" 33) NIL NIL)))) (("put" 6) (("=" 53 =) (("," 32)
                    ((":" 31) NIL NIL)
(("<" 53 <) NIL NIL)) (("if" 3) (("else" 1)((">" 53 >)
                    NIL NIL) NIL)
(("in" 4) NIL (("keys" 5) NIL NIL)))) (("to" 9)
                    (("return" 7) NIL
(("select" 8) NIL NIL)) (("[" 36) (("write" 11)
(("while" 10) NIL NIL) NIL) NIL)))) (("{}" 38 NIL)
                    NIL NIL)))
; define simpler keytable functions
(defun insert(key value)
      (setq *keytable* (binsert key value *keytable*)))
(defun lookup (key)
(blookup key *keytable*))
```

This is how the table is set up when ABC is first started. If you look for "put", you will find that the entry in *keytable* is ("put" 6), and the token list returned by the scanner is (6). This is all you need to use "put" within ABC statements. If, however, you look for "+", you will find the entry is ("+" 55 +), which returns (55 +) as the token list. The code is 55 and the + is the specified Lisp operator. You'd expect the arithmetic operators to be the same in each language; but why does "-" have the same code of 55? I'll leave you to think about that for the moment. As I create a variable such as x, it is added to the keytable as a node of the form ("x" 51 |x| "x"). Here 51 is the token code, and |x| is an interned symbol for the variable with the print name "x". (An *interned symbol* is one that is indexed by its print name in the current package, so you always get the same symbol when you ask for that print name.) The way this information is displayed may vary between versions of Common Lisp.

In Chapter 12 we investigated binary trees using numeric keys, but for our token search we must use string keys and string comparison operations. The necessary functions are defined below.

```
(defun keyentry (btree)(car btree)); Get keyed entry
                                    (key value)
(defun left(btree)(cadr btree)); Get left branch of tree
(defun right(btree)(caddr btree)); Get right branch of
                                    tree
(defun build-btree (record leftvalue rightvalue)
;Set up tree structure
      (list record leftvalue rightvalue)

(defun blookup (key btree)
```

```
;Perform binary tree search. Return NIL if key not found
(if (null btree)
     NIL
     (let ((testkey (car (keyentry btree))))
     (cond
        ((string-equal key testkey)(cdr (keyentry
                                          btree)))
        ((string-lessp key testkey)(blookup key (left
                                               btree)))
        (T (blookup key (right btree))); greater is all
                                       ; that remains
))))

(defun binsert (key value btree)
; Insert new keyed data into binary tree and return new
; tree
; Allow for value to be list or single value
(let ((record (if (atom value)(list key value)
                                     (cons key value))))
     (if (null btree); Create new binary tree structure
     (build-btree record '()'())
     (let ((testkey (car (keyentry btree))))
     (cond
        ((string-equal key testkey) ; Replace old
                                    ; value by new
           (build-btree record (left btree)(right
                                            btree)))
        ((string-lessp key testkey) ; Keep looking left!
           (build-btree (keyentry btree)
           (binsert key value (left btree)(right btree))))
        (T ; Greater so: Keep looking right!
(build-btree (keyentry btree)
           (left btree)(binsert key value (right
                                           btree))))
)))))
; Define simpler keytable functions specific to
; interpreter environment
(defun insert(key value)
     (setq *keytable* (binsert key value *keytable*)))
(defun lookup (key)
     (blookup key *keytable*))
```

It is good practice when writing code for new data structures to make it as general as possible, as I have done here. You never know when you might want to use it again. Finally, when it is debugged and well-specified, the use of simplified application-specific definitions such as **insert** and **lookup** can hide the detailed information that is unnecessary at this coding level.

Extracting Tokens

The interpreter uses **read-line** to input a string. To extract the tokens from this string the scanner looks for a character (in our case #\SPACE) which separates the tokens within the string. The string between the starting point of the search

and the space character must be a token, which I can copy to newstring for
further investigation. Once I've extracted a token from the input string, I can
check whether it is an integer. If it is, I use the Lisp function **parse-integer** to get
the number and save the integer codes and number as an element of the output
list. If the token is not a number, I check whether it's a recognizable symbol
from *keytable*, and if not return a token list specifying the token as an
unrecognized string.

I first approached the extraction of a token as the process of removing
successive characters from an input stream and passing these to an output
stream. The result was a functional but unappealing solution. In contrast the
method used here treats a string as a sequence which may be searched directly.
Using Common Lisp there are often a number of solutions to the same problem.
If you have structured your solution well, the replacement of one technique by
another should not affect the way the definition interfaces with the rest of the
application.

```
(defun scanner (instring)
; from the string extract a token sequence delimited by
; a space
(let* ((spacestring (make-sequence '(vector character)
           10:
           initial-element #\SPACE))
    (outlist NIL)(pos2 (position #\SPACE inbstring))
                 (pos1 0)
    (stringend (length instring))(newstring
              spacestring))
  (loop
(if (not pos2) (setq pos2 stringend))
; Allow for single sequence entry
          (setq newstring (subseq instring pos1 pos2))
            ; Extract string sequence
    (cond
    ; Check if the string represents an integer and
    ; convert if necessary.
          ((digit-char-p (char newstring 0))
           ; Use 50 as token value for an integer
           (push (list '50 (parse-integer newstring))
               outlist))
           ; Find any *keytable* entries
          ((lookup newstring)
           (push (lookup newstring) outlist))
           ; Must be a string value (or new variable id)
           ; with 49 as required token value
           (T (push (list '49 newstring) outlist)))
    ; Check for end of scan operations
    (if (eq pos2 stringend)(return))
; Print out the scanner result if required
(cond (*mybugs* (progn (print "SCANNER")(princ outlist))
                                        T outlist))))
    ; Update scan positions
    (setq pos1 (1+ pos2)pos2(position #\SPACE instring :
            start pos1))
  )
))
```

You can investigate the use of the scanner to convert strings to token lists as shown in the example below. With the ABC interpreter evaluated but not executing you can access the internal definitions such as the scanner. In this example I've used the version of *keytable* described above, where "fred" has not, as yet, been recognized as a variable in ABC.

```
(scanner "put 10 + 25 * ( 3 - 2 ) / 45 in fred")
((49 "fred") (4) (50 45) (56 TRUNCATE) (57) (50 2)(55 -)
(50 3) (54) (56 *) (50 25) (55 +) (50 10) ( 6))
```

Can you explain why, when you set *mybugs* true, you get the result printed out twice?

Extracting Syntax

Having scanned the input string, and created a list of token lists, I must now extract the syntax of the information in order to execute the required operations. This is quite a task, so I must first break the problem into manageable chunks. If I separate all of the algebraic operations and process them first, I can reduce the problems considerably. The function **reduce-token-list** is designed to check through the coded list received from the scanner, and to split it into two.

Each set of algebraic operations will appear as a sequence of tokens in the list, and can be separated from the rest of the information. When I find the end of an algebraic sequence, I send the list to another function **solvex** for processing, and then insert the Lisp style algebraic function back into the reduced list under the code 52, to distinguish it from other elements.

```
(defun reduce-token-list ( token-list )
(let ((reduced-list NIL) (algebraic-list NIL))
(loop
   (cond (*myerrors* (return T))
      ((and (null token-list)(not (null

                            algebraic-list)))
      (push (solvex algebraic-list) reduced-list)
         (return reduced-list))
      ((null token-list) (return reduced-list))
      ; All on the reduced list
   (T (let ((token (pop token-list)))
      (cond
      ; is it an algebraic token? If yes save it.
      ((and (< (car token) 58)(> (car token) 49))
         (push token algebraic-list))
      ; Is it a new start to the algebraic list?
((null algebraic-list) (push token reduced-list))
      ; If only one item on algebraic list return
      ; as the value
      ((null (cdr algebraic-list))(push (pop
                            algebraic-list)
         reduced-list)(push token reduced-list))
      ; otherwise process as an algebraic expression
         (T (push (solvex algebraic-list)
                  reduced-list)
```

```
              (push token reduced-list)
              (setq algebraic-list NIL))))))
    (cond (*mybugs* (print "Reduced-token-list")
        (princ reduced-list)
        (T reduced-list))
))
```

Stacks Revisited

Another use of stacks is to provide a framework for compilers and interpreters to manipulate algebraic functions. Humans normally write algebraic expressions with the operators ($+$, $-$ etc.) between the operands. For example in BASIC or Pascal you'll find expressions like:

```
A+B*C(D+E)/10 + C
```

Neither the computer nor Lisp actually handles the expression in this way. If I want to translate from a language that uses $A+B$ to a language that uses $(+\ A\ B)$, and still get the correct result, then I can use stacks to store the variables and operators temporarily, as I manipulate them into the correct form.

Furthermore, operators are not created equal. There are priority rules to be obeyed. These rules also extend to other operators including those used in "if" statements, but we shall consider only arithmetical operations here.

The scanner has provided us with a way to convert an input string to a list of numeric tokens, with additional information where needed. We haven't explained why we used the same code for different arithmetic operators. Now all will be revealed: the token code defines the precedence value. This simplifies many tests within the definitions— a very useful application of numeric token codes.

A language interpreter must be able to define functions for later use rather than immediate calculator-style execution. You may have wondered why no token value of 52 appears in the table. I've reserved it to represent an arithmetical expression which, when evaluated, will be stacked. At the end, the "evaluation" of the algebraic expression will return the token 52 with the full expression in Lisp attached. This expression is then passed on to the rest of the syntax analyser.

Optimization

An interesting side issue arises here. Commands in loops are executed repeatedly but are commonly translated every time by the interpreter. For example, an expression such as $2*3*x$ takes longer to execute than $6*x$. Is it worth making the interpreter look for such things? In other words, should we try to optimize the code? The problem is that optimization itself takes up time, so it may not be worth the time it wastes.

Our intepreter will in fact perform a certain amount of optimization, using the function **solvex**. When provided with a token-based list of variables, constants and operators, **solvex** returns a new list which has the operations correctly structured for Lisp, and simplified where possible.

Solvex is in principle quite simple. It creates two stacks, one to hold the variables and one to hold the operators. It then calls a recursive function **solve** to handle the operations on the token-based list. If the final result is just a number, then the result is returned with the code of 50; otherwise it must be an arithmetic expression, with the code of 52.

Solve is also relatively simple. If the token list is NIL, then all the unused operators must be on the operator stack. I can therefore empty it using **emptystack**, which repeatedly calls **stackeval** until there are no more operators left. Otherwise I call **checktoken** to decide what must be done with the next token in the list, and subsequently **solve** the rest of the list.

Stackeval looks at the top two operands on the variable stack and determinines whether they are both numeric. If so, it uses the Lisp evaluator to determine the value of the Lisp list built from the operator at the top of the operator stack and the two operands. For example, if the operands are 20 and 30 and the operator is * then the list (* 20 30) is built and evaluated to return 600. Alternatively, if there are variables on the variable stack, a Lisp structure is built; but instead of being evaluated, the structure itself is stored on the top of the variable stack.

```
; Polish Notation function evaluation with tokens
; Any variable used in an expression must have been
; previously initialised
(defun solvex (tlist)
    (let((VariableStack NIL)(OperatorStack NIL))
    ; Routine to obtain the value of a token precedence
    ; arithmetic list
    (cond (*mybugs* (print "SOLVEX INPUT")(princ tlist)))
        (defun solve (tlist)
        ; recursive function using the stacks of solvex.
            (defun checktoken (tokenlist)
            ; tokenlist comprises a token and any
            ; subsidiary information
            ; started at 50 to match the scanner
            ; (value, variable name or operator)
                (let((token (car tokenlist)))
                ; Check if token represents number
                (50),variable(51), or operator(53-57),
                ; 53 <, 53 =, 53 > 54 (, 55 +, 55 -,
                    56 *, 56 /, 57 ),
                ; 52 reserved for an arithmetic
                ; expression
                ; 49 is a string or undefined variable
                ; name
                (cond
                    ; If a number stack the value
                    ((= token 50)(push (cadr tokenlist)
                        VariableStack))
                    ; If a variable stack all the
                    ; information
                ((= token 51)(push tokenlist
                    VariableStack))
                    ; If an opening bracket push it onto
                    ; the operator stack
```

```
          ((= token 54)(push tokenlist
            OperatorStack))
            ; If closing bracket evaluate to
            ; balance brackets
            ((= token 57)(evaluate tokenlist))
            ; If the operator stack is empty
            ; enter the first value
        ((null OperatorStack)
          (push tokenlist OperatorStack))
            ; If the token indicates an operator
            ; precedence
            ; > tos then stack the operator
            ((> token (car(tos OperatorStack)))
              (push tokenlist OperatorStack))
            ; else evaluate expression
            (T (evaluate tokenlist)))))
(defun stackeval ()
; Take an operator and variables from the stacks and
; save the numeric expression on the variable
; stack.
; if the expression is purely numeric evaluate it.
      (let ((op2 (pop VariableStack))
            (op1 (pop VariableStack)))
        (cond
            ; Solve numeric functions if not a
            ; comparison operator
            ((and (numberp op2)(numberp op1)
                  (not (equal 53 (caar
                            OperatorStack))))
            (push (eval(list (cadr(pop
        OperatorStack)) op1 op2))
              VariableStack))
            ; Otherwise save the function as an
            ; expression
            (T (push (list (cadr(pop OperatorStack))
                            op1 op2)
              VariableStack)))))

(defun evaluate (operatortoken)
; Evaluate an expression from the stack and
; recurse on operator precedence
        ; If the operator stack is empty enter the
        ; first value
        (if (null OperatorStack)
            (push operatortoken OperatorStack)
            (let ((token (car operatortoken))
                  (stacktoken (car (tos
                            OperatorStack))))
  (cond
            ((and (= stacktoken 54)(= token 57))
            ; Opening & closing brackets
            (pop OperatorStack)) ; Remove
            ((= token 57)(stackeval)(evaluate
                            operatortoken))
            ; Start execution
```

```
                    ((> token stacktoken)
                        (push operatortoken OperatorStack))
                    (T (stackeval)(evaluate
                                operatortoken))))))
        (defun emptystack ()
        ; Clean up the stack at the end leaving one value on
        ; the variable stack
                (loop
                    (cond
                        ((null OperatorStack)(return NIL)))
                (stackeval)))
        ; Innards of solve
                (cond
                    ((null tlist)(emptystack))
                    ; Finish and return expression
                    (T (checktoken (car tlist))(solve
                                (cdr tlist)))))
        ; Innards of solvex
        (solve tlist)
                (cond
                    (*mybugs* (print "SOLVEX OUTPUT")
                        (princ VariableStack)))
                (cond
                    ((numberp (car Variablestack))
                        (list '50 (car Variablestack)))
                    (T (list '52 (car VariableStack))))))
```

The remaining functions **checktoken** and **evaluate** make use of the token codes to build and evaluate the variable and operator stacks. These functions can probably be best understood by listing the sequence of successive events in handling the token list corresponding to an arithmetic operation. For this purpose we use the expression

```
    23 + 32 * ( 3 - 2 ) / 9
```

which looks much more complicated when it is tokenized as

```
    ((50 23)(55 +)(50 32)(56 *)(54)(50 3)(55 -)(50 2)(57)
(56 TRUNCATE)(50 9))
```

The sequence of events is:

1. **Solvex** creates a variable stack and an operator stack.
2. **Solvex** calls **solve** with the token list.
3. **Checktoken** pushes 23 on to the variable stack.
4. **Solve** is called with the rest of the token list.
5. **Checktoken** pushes (55 +) onto the operator stack. Then **solve** . . .
6. **Checktoken** pushes 32 on the variable stack. Then **solve** . . .
7. * has a higher precedence than + so **checktoken** pushes (56 *) on to the operator stack. Then **solve** . . .
8. **Checktoken** always pushes the token for the opening bracket (54) on to the operator stack. Then **solve** . . .
9. **Checktoken** pushes 3 onto the variable stack. Then **solve** . . .
10. − has a higher precedence than the opening bracket so **checktoken** pushes (55 −) onto the operator stack. Then **solve** . . .

11. **Checktoken** pushes 2 onto the variable stack. Then **solve** . . .
12. **Checktoken** passes the closing bracket on to **evaluate** to determine what must be done.
13. **Evaluate** calls **stackeval** to perform the first evaluation leaving 1 as the top of the variable stack. Then **evaluate** calls itself.
14. Matching brackets are found and (54) is removed from the operator stack. Then **solve** . . .
15. *Checktoken* finds that (56 TRUNCATE) has the same precedence as (56 *) and so **evaluate** is called.
16. **Stackeval** takes the values 1 and 32 and they are multiplied with the result left on top of the variable stack. Then **evaluate** calls itself.
17. (56 TRUNCATE) has greater precedence than (55 +) so it is pushed on to the operator stack. Then **solve** . . .
18. **Checktoken** then pushes 9 on to the variable stack.
19. As the token list is now empty, **solve** calls **emptystack**.
20. **Emptystack** calls **stackeval**. **Stackeval** performs an integer division of 32 by 9 and puts the result 3 on the variable stack.
21. **Emptystack** calls **stackeval**. **Stackeval** adds 3 and 23 and puts the result 26 on the variable stack.
22. The operator stack is now empty, so **emptystack** returns to **solve**.
23. **Solve** returns to **solvex** which determines that a number has been left on the variable stack and so returns (50 26).

This illustrates how the interpreter translates statements: now all we have to do is execute them. On to the next chapter !

ABC Intepreter: Execution

---

*The executioner's argument was, that you couldn't cut off a head unless
there was a body to cut it off from: that he had never had to do such a
thing before, and he wasn't going to begin at his time of life.*

*The King's argument was, that anything that had a head could be
beheaded, and that you weren't to talk nonsense.*

*The Queen's argument was, that if something wasn't done about it in
less than no time, she'd have everybody executed, all round.*

Alice's Adventures in Wonderland

In this final chapter we'll look at an example to show how the interpreter
executes a command. I'll also write down the full code, and describe a short
interactive session using the interpreter. But first, let me state in more detail the
subset of ABC that the interpreter can handle.

What the Interpreter will Recognize

The data structures recognized by the interpreter are tables, integer variables and integer constants. The statement syntax included is shown below:

PUT {} IN FRED	Create a new table variable.
PUT whatever IN FRED ["Bill"]	Add a keyed value to a table variable.
PUT numeric value IN BERT	Create a new numeric variable.
PUT x,y, z IN z, y, x	Multiple assignment for numeric variables.
PUT algebra IN BERT	Evaluate an expression and store in a numeric variable.
WRITE FRED ["Bill"]	Print value in a table.
WRITE FRED	Print table alphabetically.
WRITE keys FRED	Print all current keys.
WRITE x, y, z	Print values of numeric variables.
. WRITE 25+33*99/(4−5)	Print result of integer calculator operations.
	Print combinations of numeric variables, strings, and newlines.
WHILE x < 100 : PUT x + 1 IN x	Loop through until condition is satisfied.
IF x = 25 : PUT y + 72 IN x	Simple conditional evaluation, <, =, >.

Plus three that are not standard ABC:

→	Provide block structure by line continuation.
QUIT	Exit from the interpreter.
;	Newline.

Template Matching

As we saw in the previous chapter, the syntax analysis must detect the statement keywords and create the corresponding Lisp expressions for subsequent evaluation. Many practical interpreters use a template matching technique which uses the keyword to select the template and then substitutes appropriately for the specific language statement used. The present interpreter uses this technique; I shall discuss its application by example rather than by exhaustive description.

Consider the ABC statement:

```
WHILE f < 100 : PUT f + y , f - y IN f , y
```

The syntax analysis (or parsing) of this statement starts at the left, and the keyword WHILE is detected. The statement structure for a WHILE is:

```
WHILE condition true EXECUTE the remaining ABC
statements.
```

An equivalent in Common Lisp is:

```
(loop (if condition (progn remaining-statements)
(return)))
```

or alternatively:

```
(loop (cond (condition remaining-statements)
            (T return)))
```

Each of these amounts to a template. I've implemented the solution using the first one. A useful exercise would be to recode the 'Whilefn' using the second approach.

After the ':' in the above example, I have to create a Lisp-executable version of the PUT statement, and then insert this into the WHILE template. Provided I can look up the symbol for the specific variable names used in the 'PUT' expressions, I can insert these into the 'PUT' template. The structure of PUTs in ABC requires that all the new values for variables be computed, and then saved in the variables, in parallel. What does this mean? In the example above consider the situation where f is equal to 9 and y is equal to 7 before the PUT statement is first executed. If I use the Lisp expression

```
(setq f (+ f y) y (- f y))
```

I'd get $f = 16$ and $y = 7$ whereas what I wanted was $f = 16$ and $y = 2$. What's the source of the problem? **Setq** is designed to evaluate the forms and assign values to the variables sequentially. What I need is a function which evaluates all the forms first and then performs the substitution. I can do this using:

```
(psetq f (+ f y) y (- f y))
```

So my Putfn template in Common Lisp becomes

```
(psetq variable expression .... )
```

If you study the listing for *syntax* given below, and the various subsidiary functions, you'll find that this technique has been applied to the numeric functions, but not always to the table operations. In order to keep the interpreter short, I've implemented the table variable functions directly, rather than retaining the flexibility inherent in the numeric operations.

The Remaining Code

```
; A function to flatten the keytable leaving (key value)
; in alphabetical order of the keys!!
(defun flatten (KTB)
  (cond
    ((null KTB) NIL)
    ((null (left KTB))(append (car KTB)(flatten (right
                                         KTB))))
    ((null (right KTB))(append (flatten (left KTB))(car
                                         KTB)))
    (T (append (flatten (left KTB))(car KTB)(flatten
                                         (right KTB)))))
  )
)
```

```
; Substitute for variables
(defun VarSub (a)
; Remove tokens
  (cond (*mybugs* (print "VarSub entry")(princ a)))
  (cond
    ((null a) NIL)
    ((and (numberp (car a))(= 50 (car a)))(cadr a))
                        ;number
    ((and (numberp (car a))(= 51 (car a)))(cadr a))
                        ;simple variable
    ((and (numberp (car a))(= 52 (car a)))(VarSub1
                        (cadr a))) ; expression
    (T (print "Error in algebraic expression") T)
  )
)

(defun VarSub1 (a)
; Do the substitutions
  (cond
    ((null a) NIL)
    ((and (numberp (car a))(= 51 (car a))(symbolp
                        (cadr a))
        (not (null (cadr a))))(cadr a))
    ((atom (car a))(cons (car a)(VarSub1 (cdr a))))
    (T (cons (VarSub1 (car a))(VarSub1 (cdr a))))
  )
)

; My own search routine at the top level only
; Return NIL if not found at all
(defun search1 (token tokenlist)
  (do ((n 0 (1+ n)))
  (NIL)
  (cond
    ((null tokenlist) (return NIL))
    ((equal token (car tokenlist))(return n))
    (T(pop tokenlist))))
  )
)

(defun search2 (token tokenlist)
; Recursive search with no information about position
  returned
  (cond
    ((null tokenlist) NIL)
    ((equal token (car tokenlist)) T)
    ((atom (car tokenlist))(search2 token (cdr
                        tokenlist)))
    (T (or (search2 token (car tokenlist))
      (search2 token (cdr tokenlist))))
  )
)
(defun set-numvar (variablename value)
; Create new variable in *keytable*
```

```
    (setq *keytable* (insert variablename (list '51
      (intern variablename) variablename)))
    (set (cadr (lookup variablename)) value)) ; Save the
                           ; value

(defun VarName (source)
; Get the variable from the token
    (cadr source)
)


; Define the structures for PUT
(defun putfn (a)
; find out the kind of variable to be used
    (let ((inpos+ (1+ (search1 '(4) a))))
    ; get the first variable position
    (defun putfn2 ( a ) ; Create the variable value list
(cond
    ((null a) NIL) ; finished
    ((= 4 (caar a)) NIL) ; in
    ((= 30 (caar a))(progn (pop a)(putfn2 a))) ; comma
    (T (cons (VarName (nth inpos+ a))
      (cons(VarSub(pop a))(putfn2 a)))))))
(cond
    ((= 51 (car (nth inpos+ a)))
    ; number type variables return an executable list
      (if (search1 '(33) a)
        (list 'progn (cons 'psetq (putfn2 a)) '(33))
        (cons 'psetq (putfn2 a))))
      ; Check and retain continuation token
    ; a table variable that exists already
    ((= 48 (car (nth inpos+ a)))
      (progn (insert (caddr (nth inpos+ a))
      (cons '48 (cons (binsert (cadr (nth (+ 2 inpos+) a))
                                  (tos a)
        (cadr (nth inpos+ a)))(cddr (nth inpos+ a))))) T))
    ; new variable determine token number from syntax
    ((= 49 (car (nth inpos+ a)))
(cond
    ((= '38 (caar a))(progn (insert (cadr (nth inpos+ a))
      (cons '48 (cons NIL (cdr (nth inpos+ a)))))T))
    ; Empty list token {}
    (T (set-numvar (cadr (nth inpos+ a)) (cadr (pop a)))
    (if (= 30 (caar a))(pop a)(return T)))
    ; Check for commas
    ))) ; initialise numeric variable
    (T (print "Error in variable type")
      (setq *myerrors* T))
    )))


; Define structures for WRITE
(defun leave-keys (tablevar)
; remove every third value in the table. Very structure-
    ; specific
    (let ((newvar '()))
    (loop
```

```lisp
      (cond ((null tablevar)(return ( reverse newvar))))
    (push (pop tablevar) newvar)
    (pop tablevar)(pop tablevar))
))

(defun writefn (a)
   (let ((writelist NIL))
      (loop (if (null a)(return (cons 'progn (reverse
                               writelist)))
 (let* ((tokenlist (pop a))(token (car tokenlist)))
    (cond
      ; Continuation token
      ((= 33 token)(push '(33) writelist))
      ((= 30 token) T) ; comma
      ; A number or a variable
      ((or(= 50 token)(= 51 token))
         (push (list 'format 'T '"~8@A" (cadr tokenlist))
                    writelist))
      ; An algebraic expression
      ((= 52 token)(push (list 'format 'T '"~8@A"
         (VarSub tokenlist)) writelist))
      ; A table
      ((= 48 token)
         (cond
            ((null a)(push (list 'princ (list 'quote
            (remove '50 (flatten2 (cadr tokenlist)))))
                           writelist))
      ((= 36 (car (tos a)))
         (push (list 'format 'T '"~8@A" (cadr(blookup (cadadr
a) cadr tokenlist)))) writelist)(return (cons 'progn
(reverse writelist))))
      (T (print "Error in table lookup")(setq *myerrors*
                       T))))
     ; A string
     ((= 49 token)(push (list 'princ (cadr tokenlist))
       writelist))
     ; The keys of a table
     ((= 5 token)(push (list 'princ (list 'quote (leave-keys
     (flatten2 (cadr (pop a))))))) writelist))
     ; Newline indicator
     ((= 32 token)(push '(terpri) writelist))
     ; used for newline rather than /
     (T (print "Error in write list")(setq *myerrors*
                       T)))))))))

; functions for IF
(defun iffn (a)
   (if *mybugs* (progn (print "iffn")(print a)))
   (list 'if (VarSub(pop a))(progn (pop a)(syntax1 a))))

; functions for WHILE
(defun whilefn (a)
   (if *mybugs* (progn (print *whilefn*)(print a)))
   (list 'loop (list 'if (VarSub (pop a)) (progn (pop a)
   (syntax1 a))'(return)))))
```

```
(defun syntax (a)
  (let ((temp NIL))
  (if *mybugs* (progn (print "Syntax")(princ a)))

(defun syntax1 (a)
  (if (null a) NIL
    (let* ((tokenterm (pop a))(token (car tokenterm)))
      (cond
      ((= token 6)(putfn a))
      ((= token 50)(writefn (push tokenterm a)))
        ; Algebraic
      ((= token 11)(writefn a))
      ((= token 3)(iffn a))
      ((= token 10)(whilefn a))
      (T (Print "Error in Syntax")(setq *myerrors* T)))))))

; internals of syntax
; check and save "→". This provides line continuation
(setq temp (syntax1 a))
  (cond (*mybugs* (print "End of Syntax")(princ temp)))
  (cond ((atom temp) temp)
  (*mysave* (setq temp (subst temp '(33) *mysave* :test
                    #'equal))
  (setq *mysave* NIL) temp)
    ((search2 '(33) temp)(setq *mysave* temp) T)
  (T temp))
))
```

A Session with the Interpreter

I'll finish by taking you through a short interactive session with the interpreter, with *mybugs* set to true. See if you can follow the operations of the interpreter through this listing.

```
? (setq *mybugs* T)
T
? (abc)
This is the ABC Interpreter
ABC> put 0, 0 in f, c
   "SCANNER" ((49 c) (30) (49 f) (4) (50 0) (30) (50 0)
             (6))
   "Reduced-token-list" ((6) (50 0) (30) (50 0) (4) (49 f)
                         (30) (49 c))
   "Syntax" ((6) (50 0) (30) (50 0) (4) (49 f) (30) (49
             c))
   "End of Syntax" T
   "EXECUTE" T
   ABC> while f < 40 : put f + 5 , 5 * ( f - 27 ) / 9 in f ,
c  →
   "SCANNER" ((33) (51 c c) (30) (51 f f) (4) (50 9) (56
TRUNCATE) (57) (50 27) (55 -) (51 f f) (54) (56 *) (50
5) (30) (50 5) (55 +) (51 f f) (6) (31) (50 40) (53 <)
(51 f f) (10))
```

```
   "SOLVEX INPUT" ((50 5) (56 *) (54) (51 f f) (55 -) (50
27) (57) (56 TRUNCATE) (50 9))
   "SOLVEX OUTPUT" ((TRUNCATE (* 5 (- (51 f f) 27)) 9))
   "SOLVEX INPUT" ((51 f f) (55 +) (50 5))
   "SOLVEX OUTPUT" ((+ (51 f f) 5))
   "SOLVEX INPUT" ((51 f f) (53 <) (50 40))
   "SOLVEX OUTPUT" ((< (51 f f) 40))
   "Reduced-token-list" ((10) (52 (< (51 f f) 40)) (31)
(6) (52 (+ (51 f f) 5)) (30) (52 (TRUNCATE (* 5 (- (51 f
f) 27)) 9)) (4) (51 f f) (30) (51 c c) (33))
   "Syntax" ((10) (52 (< (51 f f) 40)) (31) (6) (52 (+ (51
f f) 5)) (30)(52 (TRUNCATE (* 5 (- (51 f f) 27)) 9)) (4)
(51 f f) (30) (51 c c) (33))
   "Whilefn" ((52 (< (51 \f "f") 40)) (31) (6) (52 (+ (51 \f
"f") 5)) (30) (52 (TRUNCATE (+ 5 (- (51 \f "f") 27)) 9)) (4)
(51 f "f") (30) (51 c "c") (33))
   "VarSub entry" (52 (< (51 f f) 40))
   "VarSub entry" (52 (+ (51 f f) 5))
   "VarSub entry" (52 (TRUNCATE (* 5 (- (51 f f) 27)) 9))
   "End of Syntax" (LOOP (IF (< f 40) (PROGN (PSETQ f (+ f
5) c (TRUNCATE (* 5 (- f 27)) 9)) (33)) (RETURN)))
   "EXECUTE" T
   ABC> write f , Fahrenheit , c , Centigrade ;
   "SCANNER" ((32) (49 Centigrade) (30) (51 c c) (30) (49
Fahrenheit) (30) (51 f f) (11))
   "Reduced-token-list" ((11) (51 f f) (30) (49
Fahrenheit) (30) (51 c c) (30) (49 Centigrade) (32))
   "Syntax" ((11) (51 f f) (30) (49 Fahrenheit) (30) (51 c
c) (30) (49 Centigrade) (32))
   "End of Syntax" (PROGN (FORMAT T ~8aA f) (PRINC
Fahrenheit) (FORMAT T ~8aA c) (PRINC Centigrade)
(TERPRI))
   "EXECUTE" (LOOP (IF (< f 40) (PROGN (PSETQ f (+ f 5) c
(TRUNCATE (* 5 (- f 27)) 9)) (PROGN (FORMAT T ~8aA f)
   (PRINC Fahrenheit) (FORMAT T ~8aA c) (PRINC Centigrade)
   (TERPRI))) (RETURN)))
   5Fahrenheit -15Centigrade
   10Fahrenheit -12Centigrade
   15Fahrenheit -9Centigrade
   20Fahrenheit -6Centigrade
   25Fahrenheit -3Centigrade
   30Fahrenheit -1Centigrade
   35Fahrenheit 1Centigrade
   40Fahrenheit 4Centigrade
ABC> quit
   "End of the ABC Interpreter"
```

Quick Reference Guide

While the Beaver confessed with affectionate looks
  More eloquent even than tears,
It had learned in ten minutes far more than all books
  Would have taught it in seventy years.

The Hunting of the Snark

This is not an exhaustive list of Common Lisp functions and features. It includes only those dealt with earlier in this book and is intended as a convenient 'memory jogger' rather than a definitive dictionary. Also, completeness has been sacrificed for clarity in some of the definitions. If you want a detailed reference text, I suggest you refer to *'Common Lisp'* by Guy Steele, published by Digital Press.

Notation

Most of the terms employed arc sclf-cxplanatory. For example, if an argument to a function can only be a string, it is shown as 'string'. The following abbreviations are used:

a-list   association list
arg   argument
numeric-arg   numeric argument
var   variable

Angle braces are used to indicate optional repetition. Thus

<args> can be expanded into arg1 arg2 arg3, and
<(names defs)> can be expanded into (name1 def1)(name2 def2)

Function	Description
(+ <numeric-args>)	returns the sum of its arguments. e.g. (+ 3 8 6 1) returns 18.
(− <numeric-args>)	returns the difference of the first argument and the sum of all subsequent arguments. e.g. (− 7 2 1) returns 4.
(> <numeric-args>)	returns T if its arguments are in strict descending order. e.g. (> 5 2 1) returns T.
(< <numeric-args>)	returns T if its arguments are in strict ascending order. e.g. (< 3 6 8 7 9) returns NIL.
(>= <numeric-args>)	returns T if its arguments are in descending order, allowing equalities. e.g. (>= 5 5 4 4 4 3) returns T.
(<= <numeric-args>)	returns T if its arguments are in ascending order, allowing equalities. e.g. (<= 3 4 4 4 5 5) returns T.
(= <numeric-args>)	returns T if its arguments are all equal. e.g. (= 5 5 5 5) returns T.
(1+ numeric-arg)	returns numeric-arg + 1. e.g (1+ 7) returns 8.
(1− numeric-arg)	returns numeric-arg − 1. e.g (1− 7) returns 6.
(acons key data a-list)	returns (key.data) consed with a-list. e.g. (acons 'symbol '! '(number.123) (letters.*abc*)) returns ((symbol.!)(number.123)(letters.*abc*)).
(and <args>)	returns T only if each argument is T. e.g. (and T T T NIL T) returns NIL.
(append list object)	returns a list with object appended to list. e.g.(append '(x y) '(p q r)) returns (x y p q r).
(apply function list)	returns the result of applying the function to the list. e.g. (apply '+ '(1 2 3)) returns 6.
(aref array index)	returns the indexth element of array. e.g. (aref x 3).
(assoc key a-list)	returns a dotted pair consisting of key and the data associated with key in the a-list. e.g. (assoc 'letters '((number.123)(letters.*abc*))) returns (letters.abc).
(atom object)	returns T if object is an atom, NIL otherwise. e.g. (atom 'x) returns T.

Function	Description
(break control-string <args>)	suspends execution with a message defined by control-string and <args> as for format. e.g. (break "~%x is ~A" x)
(car list)	returns the head of list. e.g. (car '(a b c)) returns a.
(case var (object <actions>). . (object <actions>))	executes <actions> for the first object which contains var. e.g. (case x (1 (format T "1")(2 (format T "2"))))
(cdr list)	returns the tail of list. e.g. (cdr '(a b c)) returns (b c).
(char string index)	returns the indexth element of the array string. e.g. (char "abcd" 1) returns \/b.
(cond (pred fn) . . (pred fn))	returns the value of fn corresponding to the first predicate whose value is T. e.g.(cond ((zerop x) 'Z) (T NIL)) returns Z if x is zero, NIL otherwise.
(cons object list)	returns the list whose head is object and whose tail is list. e.g. (cons 'a '(b c d)) returns (a b c d).
(defmacro name (<args>) (replacement))	(name <args>) is replaced by replacement at run time. e.g. (defmacro double(x)(list '* x 2))
(defstruct name <elements>)	defines a structure called name to have elements. e.g. (defstruct shoe size colour sole upper) creates a structure called shoe with elements size colour sole and upper.
(defun name (<args>) (list))	returns name, having stored a function definition. The list defines the function and args is its set of formal arguments.
(do (<(var init step)> (test result) <executable-forms>)	performs a sequence of iterations of <executable-forms>. var is set to init on entry and step revises it at the end of the loop, which is repeated until test is T. Result is then returned.
(dolist (var list result) <executable-forms>)	performs iterations of <executable-forms> for all var = element-of-list (in order, head first). Returns result.
(dotimes (var limit result) <executable-forms>)	performs iterations of <executable-forms> for var = 0 to limit-1, after which result is returned.
(eq object object)	returns T if both objects are the same. (i.e. the pointers to both objects are the same.) e.g. (eq 'x 'x) returns T but (eq 3 3) may not.
(eql object object)	returns T if eq is T, or if its arguments are identical numbers or characters. e.g. (eql 123 123.0) returns NIL.
(equal object object)	returns T if both objects are structurally similar (i.e. if their printed representations are the same). e.g. (equal '((a b)(c d e)) '((a b)(c d e))) returns T.
(eval object)	returns what the object evaluates to. e.g. (eval x) returns 3, if $x = 3$
(export var)	allows var to be referenced outside its home package. e.g. (export 'x)
(flet (<(names (<args>) definitions)> body)	allows the definitions of the functions names to be restricted to the scope of the flet. e.g.(flet((x2(x)(* x 2)))(format T "~A"(x2 3)))
(format stream control-string <args>)	prints args to stream as defined by control-string. See below for format directives.
(funcall function <args>)	returns the result of function applied to <args>. e.g. (funcall '+ 1 2 3) returns 6.
(if predicate form-t form-nil)	returns form-t if predicate returns T, form-nil otherwise. e.g. (if (= 2 2) 'x 'y) returns X.
(in-package string)	transfers to the package string. e.g. (in-package "mytests")
(let (<(vars values)>) body)	binds vars to values in parallel and then executes body. e.g. (let ((x 1)(y 2))(format T "~A~A" x y))

Function	Description
(let* (<(vars values)>) body)	binds vars to values sequentially and then executes body. e.g. (let* ((x 1)(y x))(format T "~A~A" x y))
(list object)	returns (object). e.g. (list 'x) returns (x).
(load string)	The file named string is loaded from disk. If the load is successful T is returned.
(loop <forms>)	executes forms repeatedly. Exit from loop must be explicit.
(macroexpand macro)	returns the expansion of the macro. e.g. (macroexpand '(double 7)) returns (* 7 2) for the example given with defmacro.
(make-array size)	allows an array to be dimensioned. e.g. (setq a (make-array 5)) sets up an array a with indexes 0 . . 4.
(mapcar function list <lists>)	returns a list formed by applying function to successive corresponding elements of list and lists (depending how many arguments function takes). e.g. (mapcar #'abs '(2 −3 4 −7)) returns (2 3 4 7)
(merge-pathnames filename)	returns a pathname providing a link between the filename and the file system. e.g. (merge-pathnames "data.new").
(mod number m)	returns number mod m. e.g. (mod 15 4) returns 3.
(null object)	returns T if object is the empty list, NIL otherwise. e.g. (null '(a c)) returns NIL.
(numberp object)	returns T if object is a number, NIL otherwise. e.g. (numberp 5) returns T.
(or <args>)	returns T if any of its arguments is T. e.g. (or NIL NIL NIL T T NIL T) returns T.
(pairlis key-list data-list)	returns a list of dotted pairs linking corresponding elements of key-list and data-list. e.g.(pairlis '(number letters) '(123 abc)) returns ((number.123) (letters.abc))
(princ object)	prints a Lisp object. A stream may be specified as a second argument.
(print object)	prints a Lisp object. A stream may be specified as a second argument. A newline precedes the print.
(prog1 body)	executes body and returns the result of its first function. e.g. (prog1 (+ 3 4) (− 5 2) (1+ 5)) executes all three functions and returns 7.
(prog2 body)	as prog1, but returns the result of the second function. e.g. (prog2 (+ 3 4) (− 5 2) (1+ 5)) executes all three functions and returns 3.
(progn body)	as prog1, but returns the result of the last function. e.g. (progn (+ 3 4) (− 5 2) (1+ 5)) executes all three functions and returns 6.
(psetq <vars values>)	assigns values to vars in parallel. e.g. (psetq x 3 y 7 r 12) assigns 3,7 and 12 to x, y and r respectively.
(quote arg)	returns arg. e.g. (quote x) returns the symbol x.
(rassoc data a-list)	returns a dotted pair consisting of data and the key associated with data in the a-list. e.g. (rassoc 'abc '((number.123) (letters.abc))) returns (letters.abc).
(read)	returns an object delimited by white space from the keyboard.
(read-char)	returns the next character from the keyboard. A stream may be specified as an argument.
(read-line)	returns a line from the keyboard (i.e. the only delimiter is RETURN. A stream may be specified as an argument.

Function	Description
(return object)	exits a block and returns object.
	e.g. (return T)
(reverse flat-list)	returns flat-list with its elements in reverse order.
	e.g. (reverse '(a b c d)) returns (d c b a).
(setf place value)	returns value, having updated to value the location pointed to by place.
	e.g. (setf x 3) returns 3 and binds x to 3.
(setq <var value>)	returns value, having bound value to var.
	e.g. (setq x 3) returns 3 and binds x to 3.
(string= string string)	returns T if both strings are identical.
	e.g. (string= "Brown" "brown") returns NIL.
(string< string string)	returns T if the first string is less than the second.
	e.g. (string< "able" "baker") returns T.
(string> string string)	returns T if the first string is greater than the second.
	e.g. (string> "able" "baker") returns NIL.
(string<= string string)	returns T if the first string is less than or equal to the second.
	e.g. (string<= "able" "able") returns T.
(string>= string string)	returns T if the first string is greater than or equal to the second.
	e.g. (string>= "able" "able") returns T.
(string/= string string)	returns T if the first string is not equal to the second.
	e.g. (string/= "able" "baker") returns T.
(string-equal string string)	returns T if both strings are equal, ignoring case.
	e.g. (string-equal "Brown" "brown") returns T.
(string-capitalize string)	returns string with initial letters upper case.
	e.g. (string-capitalize "mr smith") returns Mr Smith.
(string-downcase string)	returns string in lower case.
	e.g. (string-downcase "UPPER") returns "upper".
(string-upcase string)	returns string in upper case.
	e.g. (string-upcase "lower") returns "LOWER".
(terpri)	prints a newline. A stream may be specified as an argument.
(unless predicate <forms>)	returns NIL if predicate is T. Otherwise forms are evaluated.
	e.g. (unless (<bill 20000)
	(format T "Cannot pay")).
(unread-char char)	returns the last read character to the input buffer for re-reading. A stream may be specified as a second argument.
(when predicate <forms>)	executes forms if predicate is T.
	e.g. (when (> x 20) (format T "x is too large")
	(setq x 0))
(with-open-file (stream pathname options) body)	opens a file for actions defined by options. The defaults will open the file for input, expect characters and flag an error if the file does not exist. Stream defines the stream to be used by read etc. in body. Pathname is usually defined by a call to merge-pathnames. Body is then executed with the file open. The file is closed on exit.
(write-char char)	prints a character. A stream may be specified as a second argument.
(write-string string)	prints string. A stream may be specified as a second argument.
(y-or-n-p string)	prints string as a prompt and returns T or NIL depending on whether 'y' or 'n' is entered at the keyboard. The function is not case sensitive.
	e.g. (y-or-n-p "Do you want IBM compatibility?").
(zerop number)	returns T if number is zero, NIL otherwise.
	e.g. (zerop 12) returns NIL.

"Is that all?" Alice timidly asked.
"That's all," said Humpty Dumpty. "Goodbye."

Through the Looking-Glass

Subject Index